The Formative Years

CANADA 1812-1871

ILLUSTRATIONS BY C.W. JEFFERYS

THE RYERSON PRESS   TORONTO

Published by The Ryerson Press, Toronto, Canada, September, 1968. The Formative Years is reprinted with the permission of Imperial Oil Limited, 111 St. Clair Avenue West, Toronto 7, Ontario from the *Imperial Oil Review*, July, 1967. The drawings and paintings illustrating this edition are copyrighted and may not be reproduced without permission.

Cover/Louis-Joseph Papineau
         addressing an election crowd in
         the 1830s

Editor/James Knight

Designer/W. A. Williamson

Printed and bound in Canada.

Contents

C.W. Jefferys

The man whose paintings and drawings illustrate this book is widely regarded as Canada's greatest historical artist. In a working lifetime that spanned sixty years, Charles Jefferys recorded every period of Canadian history with illustrations that are painstakingly accurate, rendered in a style that throws their details into sharp, clear focus.

Jefferys also put into his drawings a vitality that has made them more than historical records. He drew events as he imagined them to have happened, portraying real people in real moments of history. His painting of Alexander Mackenzie reaching the Pacific, for example, shows the strain of the long trip overland in the explorer's gaunt face and the exhausted poses of his tattered men. And that is the way it must have been, without flags or fanfare or upraised sword—just a band of tired men with a long journey still before them and Mackenzie alone aware of their accomplishment.

Jefferys knew the historical value of his work, and one of his last efforts was to bring it together into a single collection. He was working on this project with Imperial Oil when he died in 1951 at the age of 82. Since then the collection has grown to number approximately 1,200 drawings and paintings, including a portfolio of 102 drawings Jefferys did for an edition of Sam Slick stories. The collection is maintained today by Imperial Oil Limited, and the company makes reproductions available for cultural and educational purposes.

The Formative Years

Conflagration

by ROBERT COLLINS

The War of 1812

Battle of Lundy's Lane, 1814

IT was doomed to be one of the forgotten wars of history. For the British, at the time, it was just a minor colonial skirmish in the boondocks of North America. For the Americans, it was a defeat best forgotten as quickly as possible. For Canadians, even now, the War of 1812-14 languishes in most of our history books as a dry, inconsequential little fracas.

Yet *what* a war it was. It had everything: trickery, gallantry, atrocities; Indians, redcoats, battleships, cavalry charges; cowards, heroes, and bunglers. It was probably *the* crucial war in our history. For the first and only important time, Canada's two founding races stood together to drive an invader from their soil. Had they failed there'd be no centennial to celebrate this year. But they won and, united as never before, went on to build a country.

Canada was anything but a country then. Its mere half million people in the Maritimes, Lower Canada (now Quebec) and Upper Canada (Ontario), were strung out in handfuls on the rim of the wilderness. They had little in common except the British flag. Some were Americans, who'd arrived in the wake of the United Empire Loyalists but whose loyalty was much less certain. Nearly two thirds were French-Canadian, who still bore no particular love for Britain. All were caught in a familiar squeeze, one they'd already experienced during earlier boundary settlements: on the one hand, nearly eight million Americans, flexing their new-found muscles; on the other, mother England, collecting and hoarding pieces of Empire like so many postage stamps.

Historians still debate the real causes of the war. The superficial reasons were plain enough. Britain, locked in a death struggle with Napoleon, forbade trade with France and was strong enough at sea to enforce it. Not only did she block neutral America's trade but invoked the right to search, for British navy deserters, any merchantmen she could catch. Of the many insulting 'incidents' arising from this high-handed policy, the most outrageous came in 1807 when the British plucked some genuine American sailors from the U.S. Navy frigate *Chesapeake*, killing others in the process. No matter that Britain was wrong and apologized. From then on Americans screamed for England's blood.

Many of them—and here was an underlying cause of the war—*welcomed* the excuse to challenge England. They still hated the British, coveted Canada and thought the latter would be an easy conquest. Former president Thomas Jefferson said victory would be 'a mere matter of marching'. Future president Andrew Jackson pictured it as a 'military promenade'. Henry Clay, a warlike nationalist, trumpeted, 'I would take the whole continent from them. I wish never to see peace till we do.' The U.S. secretary of war believed war was unnecessary; a disenchanted Canada would come running to the Stars and Stripes at the first invitation.

They were all wrong, partly because they misjudged Canadians, partly because of American military blunders, partly because not all Americans wanted war. On the vote in June, 1812, the Senate was divided, 19-13; the House of Representatives, 79-49. Boston flew flags at half-mast when war was declared. New England as a whole refused to fight or buy U.S. war bonds and traded amiably with Nova Scotia and New Brunswick throughout.

But the Canadians wanted war even less. They were still struggling up from a primitive pioneer society. Communications were slow; roads were little better than trails. Particularly in Upper Canada, which was to bear the brunt of the war, the days and nights were filled with hard work and simple diversion: farming, milling, dancing, singing in the taverns, horse racing, hunting and amateur theatricals. Canadians had neither the heart nor facilities for battle.

They were shockingly outnumbered. At the outbreak, 8,000 British and Canadian regulars and less than 20,000 fighting militia stood against America's 35,000 regulars and a fluctuating rabble of militia in the hundreds of thousands. By war's end Britain and Canada had mustered a mere 125,000 fighting men to America's 575,000. All the same, Canada started with some distinct assets: discipline, training, purpose and a leader.

He was Upper Canada's General Isaac Brock, a 43-year-old career soldier with all the qualities of greatness. He was physically striking: six-foot-two with powerful shoulders, massive head and a strong shaft of a nose. He cut a fine swath in colonial society but he was no ballroom general. He had taken the Canadian posting reluctantly, yearning for the action and glory of European campaigns. But with characteristic thoroughness and fluent French learned in his native Guernsey, he studied the people and problems of the Canadas. He grew so committed to the colony that he later turned down a posting to Spain.

Brock's troops, in turn, liked him, for he was fair—a rare trait in an age when a lost tunic button could earn a soldier 50 strokes from a lash pickled in brine. He was utterly fearless and made quick, accurate decisions. He knew the future battlegrounds as no other commander did. And in a war that flickered sporadically over three distinct fronts—the Niagara peninsula and Upper Canada west, the Montreal and lower St. Lawrence region, and the Great Lakes—Brock was the standout, the first real Canadian war hero, the pace-setter for all who followed.

The Americans, for their part, set a different pattern: bungling and boneheadedness from the very beginning. Right after war's declaration, a U.S. fur trader, John Jacob Astor—more concerned about his northern trade than his patriotism—sent relays of warning riders to the British at Niagara and his agents in Montreal. Canada promptly capitalized on the tip. Captain Charles Roberts, posted high on Lake Huron, pondered conflicting orders from Canadian Governor-General Sir George Prevost ('Don't attack') and Brock ('Use your own judgment') and chose the one he liked. He moved on America's nearby Fort Michilimackinac with 45 redcoats, 180 *voyageurs* and 400 Indians. The U.S. commander was understandably surprised; the war had been on for a month but nobody'd told him. He surrendered without a shot.

Upper Canada was heartened. So were flocks of uncommitted Indians who now joined up with Canada. But not so William Hull, an aging U.S. general who'd been making forays and bloodcurdling threats across the Canadian border. He feared the scalping knife and further British attacks and he now scurried back to his headquarters at Detroit.

Meanwhile, the Canadians had captured a Yankee schooner with Hull's secret plans and evidence of dissent in his ranks. That

HOUSES of the WAR of 1812 & MAP of the NIAGARA FRONTIER

8 Miles

Main Roads —— Forts ✖
By Roads ····· Battles ✗

Gage House on Battlefield of Stoney Creek.

Looking south to Stoney Creek Battlefield. From sketch by B.J. Lossing, 1860.

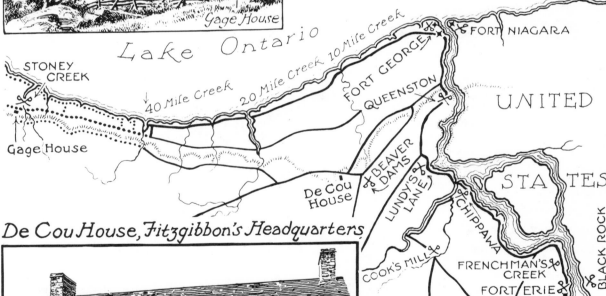

Gage House

Lake Ontario

Lake Erie

STONEY CREEK

40 Mile Creek   20 Mile Creek   10 Mile Creek

FORT GEORGE   FORT NIAGARA

QUEENSTON

UNITED

Gage House

De Cou House

BEAVER DAMS

LUNDY'S LANE

STATES

CHIPPAWA

BLACK ROCK

COOK'S MILL

FRENCHMAN'S CREEK

FORT ERIE

BUFFALO

Point Abino

Sugar Loaf Point

De Cou House, Fitzgibbon's Headquarters

C.W.J.

Private — White / Red — Belts, Lace & Buttons White — Grey

General — Red / White — Buttons & Lace Gold — White

Captain — White / Red — Grey

Sergeant — All Coats Scarlet — Red / White — White — Sashes Crimson — Trousers

C.W.J.

was enough for Brock. As the favorite ballad of the day, 'The Bold Canadian', told it:

At length our brave commander,
Sir Isaac Brock by name,
Took shipping at Niagara
And unto York he came.
Says he, 'Ye valiant heroes,
Will ye go along with me
To fight those proud Yankees
In the west of Canada?'

Brock and his force took bateaux down Lake Erie to a fort at Amherstburg. Here he met a man in his own mold: Tecumseh, a Shawnee chief, already a legend in the region. The Shawnee was 43, a tense sinewy five-foot-nine, with light copper skin and bright hazel eyes. He was a born warrior. Already with 25 braves he'd routed a Hull force of 200. Yet unlike most Indians he was compassionate. Once Tecumseh captured three of Hull's messengers, stained with walnut juice in a clumsy attempt to slip past

his scouts, but he refused to torture the phony redskins.

Now, while Brock listened quietly to reports and gave cool, quick orders, Tecumseh cried to his followers, 'Ho-o-oe, this is a *man!*' At a war council that night he backed Brock's plan of attack and carved from memory on a strip of bark a remarkably detailed map of the terrain around Fort Detroit. It was a formidable stronghold: 22-foot ramparts, a palisade of 10-foot hardwood spikes, 33 cannon and an eight-foot moat. Within were 2,000 men. Brock had 700 whites (half of whom were raw militia) and 600 Indians. But he moved down river opposite Detroit, demanded Hull's surrender, was refused.

In the morning the astonished Hull looked out to find Brock on his doorstep. It was a small but awesome force. Tecumseh had gathered a glittering array of tribes, with names that throbbed like distant war drums: Shawnee, Miami, Fox, Sac, Ottawa, Wyan-

UNIFORMS of the WAR of 1812

Grenadiers
8th, Kings,
Regiment.

Scarlet
Coat,
Blue Facings,
Dark Grey
Trousers.
Waterproof
Cap worn
over Shako
in stormy
weather

Trooper
19th Light
Dragoons
Blue, Facings Yellow.

Officer,
Light Infantry
Company,
41st Regt.
Scarlet Coat.
Green Feather
on Shako.
Gilt Chain Fringe
on shoulders.
Grey Trousers.
Curved Sabre.

Captain, U.S. Infantry, 1813.

dot, Chippewa, Potawatomi, Winnebago, Dakota. Brock's regulars were resplendent targets in scarlet tunics, grey trousers, red shakos and varying sashes, belts, braid and buttons depending on rank. The general himself was magnificent—full dress scarlet with gold lace and buttons, red cocked hat, white trousers, glistening black boots. As always he rode in front ('Other chiefs say 'Go', he says 'Come',' Tecumseh marvelled) on his splendid grey charger, Alfred. Tecumseh, on a grey mustang, rode beside him.

Hull was already unnerved. Indians frightened him. A lucky Canadian cannon shot from across the river had killed four of his men. Now, according to the ballad:

Those Yankee hearts began to ache,
Their blood it did run cold
To see us marching forward
So courageous and so bold.
Their general sent a flag to us,
For quarter he did call,
Saying, 'Stay your hand, brave British boys,
I fear you'll slay us all.'

Which is precisely what happened. Hull surrendered without a shot. Brock ceremoniously gave Tecumseh his sash and pistols, receiving in return the Shawnee's gaudy sash with woven arrow pattern. Then he turned the fort over to a subordinate, Col. Henry

General Isaac Brock lands at Detroit

C.W. JEFFERYS

ARTILLERY

Monogram & Crown
of George III on
24 Pounder

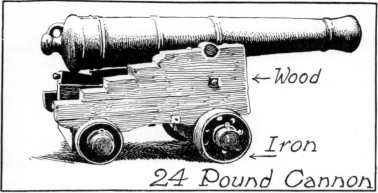

24 Pound Cannon

Short Range Ship Carronade

Bronze Field Cannon

Light
Field
Gun
Wood

Bronze Howitzer

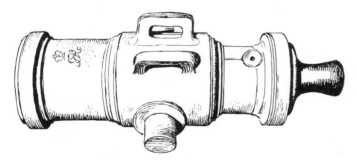

6 Pounder Field Gun

BLOCK HOUSES

Diagonal
Blockhouse ↓

At Fort York, Toronto

At
Kingston Mills to
guard Rideau Canal

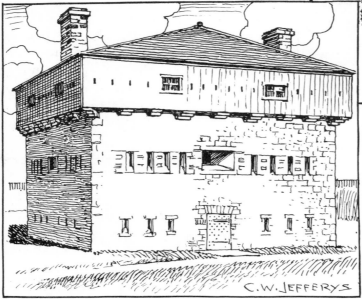

Stone Blockhouse in
Fort Wellington, Prescott, Ont.

Shingle~covered
Blockhouse in Fort
Edward, Windsor, N.S.

10

FORTS at the MOUTH of the NIAGARA

Ft. Niagara   Ft. George   Newark   Lighthouse   Battery

Procter, and returned to jubilant Upper Canada where he shrewdly attributed the victory to his 'homespun warriors'. In fact, the militia was never a really decisive factor; the trained regulars (including many Canadians) did the real fighting throughout the war. But until then, Canada's morale was at rockbottom; now it soared.

Given his head, Brock would have carried the war into other American territory. But Prevost, not noted for his military acumen, negotiated a temporary armistice in a try for peace. While it dragged on, the Americans hastily reinforced their posts. When the armistice ended, September 7, 1812, they had amassed 6,800 men to Brock's 1,700 along the 33 miles of Niagara River between Lakes Erie and Ontario. Now Brock could only wait, outnumbered and meagerly equipped,

wondering where the attack would come.

Near 4 a.m. on October 13 he sprang from his bed at Fort George to the sound of distant gunfire. He knew the enemy might strike Fort George, or Queenston Heights seven miles away, or both. He flung on his clothes, sprang to the saddle and made for the gate. A mud-splattered dragoon met him: 'Enemy crossing the river in force!' Crouched low over Alfred's neck he urged the charger down the river road. Church bells began to cry the alarm. Lights winked on in houses. Brock pounded on through the wind and drizzle, his last ride, a race to literally save Canada. Ahead he could see the flicker of cannon: his own two against the American 24. Another messenger met him. Brock waved him alongside without breaking stride and listened as they rode: Americans were swarming ashore at Queenston. 'Go back to Fort George, get General Sheaffe and all available men,' he ordered and pressed on.

He burst into Queenston in the half-light. A handful of soldiers cheered him. He galloped up the Heights which rise 345 feet over the Niagara River at this point. A single

Powder Magazine Ft. George. Built 1796.

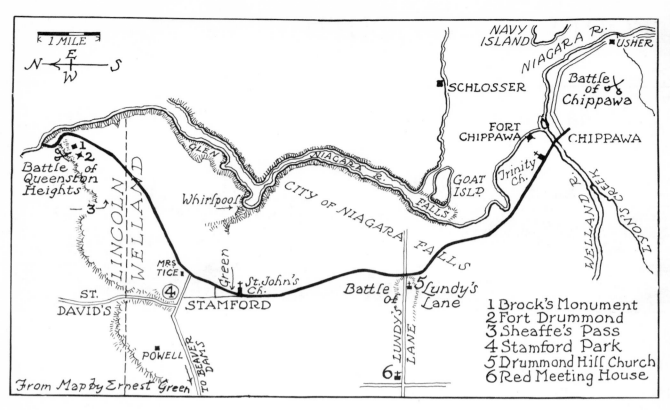

Niagara Portage Road, *an important highway for troops during War of 1812*

cannon (the other was set up a mile away) was stubbornly peppering the Americans below who'd made the easy 200-yard river crossing.

General Brock's ride to Queenston, 1812

Suddenly there were yells from the rear: 300 Yankees had found a little-known fisherman's path up the Heights, circled behind and were charging. 'Spike the gun,' cried Brock and, leading his horse, ran down-hill with the gunners.

The rain was over. In bright morning sunshine he gathered a hundred men, led them to the bottom of the hill, said, 'Take your breath, boys, you'll need it.' Then he patted Alfred apologetically for the punishing ride and, on foot, led a sword and bayonet charge up the Heights. The Americans wilted. Brock, always in front in his scarlet, caught a bullet in the wrist but ignored it. The enemy fell back to the brink of the cliff. Then an American stepped from the brush 30 yards away, took deliberate aim and shot Brock in the chest. He died almost instantly. His men, shocked and disorganized, retreated with his body.

Brock's aide, Col. John Macdonell, led another charge. Again the Americans retreated; again the Canadians' leader was

General Brock meets Shawnee Chief Tecumseh at Amherstburg

killed; again the Americans surged back. Now the Stars and Stripes floated over Queenston Heights. Two thousand militiamen prepared to cross from the opposite shore. But suddenly America's victory went sour. Sheaffe was closing in with reinforcements. Indian gunfire and warwhoops drew nearer. And the American militia—mainly noted for insolence to officers, dozing on sentry duty and going home on whim—lost its nerve. Implore as he would, American General Van Rensselaer couldn't get 2,000 of his militia to set foot on Canadian soil. The regulars and militia on the Heights were soon overpowered. Suddenly it was a smashing Canadian victory—but Brock was gone. Still, he had saved Canada, for a time at least.

His successor, Sheaffe, was a poor substitute but for a time this didn't matter. The Americans were busily fighting each other. Washington replaced the luckless Van Rensselaer with General Alexander Smyth, who scolded his militia for their shabby conduct.

Some promptly deserted. Others shot at Smyth whenever he ventured from his tent— and sometimes even when he didn't.

The next year began no better for the U.S. Procter moved out of Fort Detroit with a thousand whites and Indians, took on an equal number of Americans at Frenchtown (now Monroe, Michigan) one January dawn and won a gory victory. He took 500 prisoners and couldn't stop the Indians—still nursing old grievances against these western Yankees who'd taken their land and razed their villages — from literally butchering many of the 400 others who were killed in the fight.

But in April America finally won a campaign. A strong force sailed over Lake Ontario to York. The capital of Upper Canada wasn't much of a town: government buildings, marketplace with pillory for wrongdoers, frame houses, mills, dirt streets that turned to quagmire in the rain, and 1,200 people plus the army. The army, under floun-

First Parliament Buildings, 1796–1813.

Charles-Michel de Salaberry at Chateauguay, 1813

dering Sheaffe, was ill-prepared. Its confusion was compounded when an artilleryman accidentally dropped a lighted match in a chest of cartridges, blowing 35 men in the air.

The invaders quickly took the town. Sheaffe and his regulars retreated, setting off a powder magazine that killed 200 Americans and made them so angry they burned the Parliament Buildings. They also looted a few stores, paroled all men of military age and sailed south. A month later they took Fort George, at the junction of Lake Ontario and the Niagara River. Now the Niagara frontier was theirs. With a little effort they could

probably sever Upper Canada from the east.

But the stubborn colonials stopped them again. On June 5, after pursuing the remnants of the Fort George detachment (who had fled north to Burlington Bay), the Americans camped overnight at Stoney Creek, on the southeast edge of the present site of Hamilton. They planned to end it all the next day—but they waited one night too long. Around 2:30 a.m., outnumbered about two to one as usual, a force of 700 Canadian and British regulars attacked the enemy camp. They'd stolen the American countersign, thanks to a talkative Yankee prisoner and a sharp-eared Canadian settler, and used

Laura Secord warns Colonel Fitzgibbon of planned attack on Beaver Dam

it to silently capture the sentries. Then they took the Yankee cannon at bayonet point and the Americans retreated, disorganized, to Fort George. They were not alone in their confusion. British General John Vincent had his horse shot from under him, got lost in the woods and showed up the next morning minus hat and sword.

The Canadians advanced cautiously as far as Beaver Dam, near Queenston. Their Indians constantly harassed the enemy. Finally the Americans assigned 600 picked men to wipe out Beaver Dam. A few nights before the attack, two American officers invited themselves to dinner at the home of James Secord, a Loyalist still recovering from wounds received while fighting for Brock at

Queenston Heights. As they ate their commandeered meal, they talked of the surprise in store for Beaver Dam. Their careless talk was the beginning of a Canadian legend.

At sunrise next morning, Laura Secord, a slight 38-year-old mother of four, drove a cow casually past an American outpost, until she was out of sight, then dropped her milk pail and started a 12-mile (some sources say 20-mile) tramp through the backwoods to Beaver Dam. Avoiding main roads and dodging quick-triggered scouts she plodded through the steaming June heat, over swollen streams, through thickets of brambles until she fell tattered and exhausted among Canadian Indians. They finally took her to James Fitzgibbon, the commander. Ironically, he already had word of the attack. But her deed was no less heroic and Laura Secord was forever enshrined in the hearts and chocolate boxes of her countrymen. Soon after, the Americans marched into an Indian ambush and surrendered before the Canadian regulars fired a shot.

Farther west, Procter had come upon hard times. His presence at Detroit had been keeping all of what is now south-western Ontario out of enemy hands, but defeat was only a matter of time. His Indian forces fluctuated unpredictably, his militia had to go back to the farms, he was low on supplies, and the Americans controlled Lake Erie. In September he burned Fort Detroit and began a long retreat up the River Thames. At Moraviantown, about 70 miles upriver, Tecumseh induced him to make a stand. The Shawnee himself sensed it was the end. 'My body will

Tecumseh at the Battle of the Thames, 1813

C.W. JEFFERYS

Battle of Stoney Creek, 1813

remain on the field of battle,' he told his braves. And he died at the Battle of the Thames, October 5, 1813, in the manner of Brock: at the head of his braves, flinging a tomahawk at the American commander. As the Americans crushed his forces, Procter fled with a few men and was subsequently court-martialed. His crime was faint-heartedness but he was fighting a battle he couldn't possibly have won.

Back around Niagara the American commander of Fort George, George McClure, was making his mark in infamy. After pillaging the area during October and November, most of his men deserted for not getting paid. McClure decided to abandon the fort. At dusk on December 10 he burned Newark

(now Niagara-on-the-lake), turning 400 men, women and children into the snow.

It was the war's most wanton act and Canadian reaction was swift and terrible. McClure, while noting that 'the enemy is much exasperated', felt safe enough across the river in Buffalo. But on the night of December 19 the Canadians crossed the river and began their revenge. At 4 a.m. they silently strangled or bayoneted the sentries at Fort Niagara, swarmed inside and took it all with the bayonet. Then, under a new general, Gordon Drummond, almost the equal of Brock, they raged along the American side burning Lewiston, Fort Schlosser, Black Rock and Buffalo (where $190,000 worth of frame buildings went up in smoke).

Battle of Lake Erie, 1813

As the war moved into its final year, the Americans, with better generalship and better-trained militia, were still stubbornly determined to take the Niagara peninsula. A large part of Upper Canada was badly battered and, through various kinds of connivance, was even buying food from the American side. Drummond's 4,400 men were thinly stretched across the front, hoping to stall an attack that might come at any point.

It came, finally, out of Buffalo in early July. The enemy won a battle near Chippawa and began the long advance toward Drummond's position at Burlington, just east of present-day Hamilton. But a few miles on, still within earshot of Niagara Falls, the Americans and a Canadian army ran head-

on, to their mutual surprise, at a crossroads called Lundy's Lane. The Canadians, believing themselves hopelessly outnumbered, prepared to withdraw. Then Drummond galloped up to rally them, setting the stage for the war's bloodiest battle.

It began at 6 p.m., July 25. The odds were evener than usual: 4,000 Americans against 3,000 Canadians. The site was a long low rise, a mile from the Niagara River. The focal point was Drummond's seven-gun battery. Again and again through the evening, the battery changed hands until both sides retired exhausted and the guns stood silent and alone.

Drummond had lost a third of his men but 1,200 reinforcements stumbled into the line.

The Americans began a final assault. They took the guns. The Canadians drove them back. All through the hot black night muskets rattled, bayonets flashed, the dying screamed. The senior officers on both sides were wounded. After six bloody hours the Americans reeled back to Chippawa. The Canadians slumped on the battlefield. In the hush, the distant rumble of the Falls was heard again. Nobody had really won the battle of Lundy's Lane but Upper Canada had refused to yield.

During all of these years America's leaders repeatedly muffed a strategy that would surely have won the war: cutting off Lower Canada from Upper Canada. They talked about it in 1812 but dallied too long. Finally in September, 1813, two Yankee armies set out for Montreal, with their commanders, Wilkinson and Hampton, constantly bickering at each other.

At the Chateauguay River, 35 miles southwest of Montreal, Hampton ran into a crack French-Canadian force led by Lieutenant Colonel Charles-Michel de Salaberry, a talented strategist with the bold eye and tough jaw of an Old West gunfighter on the late late show. Any previous doubts about French-Canadian courage or loyalty were now dispelled. Outnumbered four to one, de Salaberry's force built breastworks of logs to block the main approach, carefully arranged their sparse forces and waited.

Hampton sent 1,500 of his 6,500 men to encircle the Canadians. But this advance party got lost in the dark and paused, waiting for the main force to press in. Hampton, with lost communications, waited in vain for the advance party to attack. De Salaberry spotted their confusion from atop a huge tree stump. A portion of his excellent little army checked the main enemy force at the barricades. The others wheeled on the 1,500 wandering Yankees and, with the aid of wild whoops and bugle calls which suggested a huge army, scattered the advance party in such panic that some began shooting at

each other. Hampton and his whole army turned tail.

Meanwhile Wilkinson, with more than 7,000 men, moved down the St. Lawrence with a small force snapping at his heels. This harassing squad of 1,000 men was perhaps the most cosmopolitan army ever assembled in North America. On the St. Lawrence River were Royal Navy, Provincial Marine, French-Canadian *voyageurs* and English-Canadian boatmen from the fur trading posts. On land were British regulars, Canadian regulars of both races, French-Canadian and English-Canadian militia, and a band of Indians.

On November 11 they locked with the enemy on John Crysler's farm, 20 miles west of present-day Cornwall, on the north shore. It was open ground, well-suited to the 'thin red line' shoulder-to-shoulder principle of formal infantry warfare. Most of the Canadian force had slept on the ground through a cold drizzle, and they rose in a mean temper to unlimber their flintlock muzzle-loading muskets and ram the long spike-like bayonets into place. Bayonets were the real weapon. A well-trained man could fire three rounds per minute but the loose-fitting musket ball, in a weapon with neither front nor rear sights, was apt to veer wildly off target. A hit beyond 100 yards was sheer luck.

The Americans advanced. The colonial lines—disciplined, well-drilled and cool—held fast, then forged ahead. The Americans wavered, fell back and, by night, were fleeing across the river. Later even the U.S. admitted to have taken a 'severe drubbing' at Crysler's farm.

The Americans made by far their best showing on the water. On the Atlantic, although there was no matching the British navy for sheer force, Yankee skippers did well in ship-for-ship encounters. They took 1,344 British merchantmen during the war and, in 1812 alone, won five straight duels with British warships.

Inland, after a slow start, they had things

BRITISH COMMANDERS : WAR of 1812

GENERAL BROCK

Lieut~Col. Charles
de Salaberry

Sir Gordon Drummond

AMERICAN COMMANDERS : WAR of 1812

Commodore
Isaac Chauncey

Captain
Oliver Hazard
Perry

Gen. James
Wilkinson

British and American ships clash on Lake Ontario, 1813

much their own way on the Lakes. Since these and the rivers were Canada's lifeline, the Americans could have parlayed this into total victory—but the land forces failed to follow it up.

The first showdown was on Lake Erie in 1813. There the Americans had a first-rate captain, 28-year-old Oliver Perry. For a time he was bottled up in port by the opposing fleet of Captain Robert Barclay, a one-armed veteran of Trafalgar. When Barclay finally had to withdraw for supplies, Perry slipped out and on September 10, nine American and six Canadian vessels fought it out for two hours at close quarters, sails billowing, cannon barking. Perry had one flagship shot out from under him, moved to another and won both the battle and the lake.

Events on Lake Ontario were closer to comic opera. Both commanders—Yeo for the British, Chauncey for the Americans—were able, but precious little real fighting went on. In one indecisive skirmish, which derisive onlookers called 'The Burlington Races',

Chauncey chased Yeo into Burlington Bay. On another occasion, while Chauncey and Yankee land forces invaded York, Yeo slipped down to the Americans' Lake Ontario base, Sackett's Harbor, and did some damage.

For a while both sides did more shipbuilding than fighting, in Kingston and Sackett's Harbor respectively. In May, 1814, Yeo raided Oswego on the American side (taking it handsomely) and Sackett's Harbor (losing dismally). Later that year the Canadians suffered a disastrous defeat on Lake Champlain.

By this time, though, the sheer numbers of Britain's navy were effectively blockading the whole American east coast. The Yankee ports were slowly smothering and American victories on the Lakes or even, ship-for-ship, on the Atlantic, meant nothing in the end. And now, with Napoleon finally out of the way, Britain shook itself like a weary mastiff and turned around to properly deal with the pesky Americans.

In mid-August a British fleet sailed into Chesapeake Bay, headed for Washington with 4,000 troops aboard. A small American naval force fell back before them, finally burning its vessels and taking to land. On August 24, 6,000 American troops formed up at Bladensburg, north of Washington. President Madison rode out to watch the show, but it was a short-short feature. In the first skirmish eight Americans were killed, 11 wounded and 5,000 militiamen ran for their lives. The British easily captured the regulars who stood their ground.

That night in orderly fashion, the British marched unmolested into the capital of an area theoretically defended by 93,500 militia. They harmed no person or private property but, in reprisal for York, partly burned the government buildings and the presidential mansion. President and Dolly Madison left so abruptly that the redcoats found their unfinished dinner on the table. Then, having slapped America's wrist, the British marched back to their boats. (The campaign was not a *total* loss for America: the mansion, repainted to cover the smoke stains, became known evermore as the White House. And three weeks later, as the British unsuccessfully shelled a fort near Baltimore, failing to bring down the flag, onlooker Francis Scott Key wrote 'The Star Spangled Banner'.)

The exercise demonstrated rather clearly that Britain, with additional effort, might have taken America back again or at least named its own terms in the post-war settlement. But it had enough problems elsewhere and let itself be out-negotiated at the Treaty of Ghent. In fact, the treaty was more of an armistice; details of peace were worked out in agreements over subsequent years.

In 1817 the Great Lakes were demilitarized and no naval forces permitted to be maintained on them. This contributed to peace between the nations in the years ahead. In 1818 the western boundary and fishery problems were settled. The old boundary line became firm: the 49th parallel from Lake of the Woods to the Rockies. In a vague fisheries arrangement that was to plague Canada for nearly a century after, the Yankees lost their right to fish and cure their catch along the Nova Scotia coast but were allowed the use of certain other Atlantic shores.

No word about the causes of the war was incorporated in the treaty. And even though Britain had taken northern Maine, the pre-war boundaries were reinstated. The only visible result of the war was the terrible condition of parts of Upper Canada: poverty stricken, ravaged, partly destroyed.

The silly, cruel and wasteful war ended officially on Christmas Eve, 1814. But it was not a complete waste. Never again did the Americans actually take arms against Canada. And the Canadian spirit was intact; was, in fact, for the first time a strong identifiable thing. By holding fast in the War of 1812 Canada took a long step toward nationhood.

Specialized research for this article was contributed by Graeme Bacque

An election in the 1830s during the struggle for Responsible Government

Agitation

by ARTHUR R. M. LOWER, *Professor Emeritus of History, Queen's University*

The struggle for self-rule

In the British North America of 1820, there were only a few hundred thousand people loosely strung out on the long line from Gaspé to Lake Huron, plus smaller contingents in Nova Scotia and New Brunswick. The country was nowhere more than a few miles thick. Only four places could be dignified with the term 'city'—Quebec, Montreal, Halifax, Saint John—and none of these was impressive. A road of sorts stretched between Quebec and the peninsula of Upper Canada, but it was secondary and the only way up country of any carrying capacity was by the river and the lakes.

The apparatus of civilized life was almost as meager as communications were poor. French Canada, it is true, had long had its institutions of education for its *élite* and Nova Scotia and New Brunswick were making a beginning. But, save for one or two 'schools for the sons of gentlemen', Upper Canada had little in the way of educational apparatus. All the provinces, however, had a vigorous local press, which argues that a considerable proportion of the population could read and write. Except for the newspapers that came their way, most people were not much interested in reading and writing, anyway; they were interested in cutting down trees, burning them up, sowing and reaping, getting through the winter and, with what energy was left over, perhaps roistering at the local tavern or assuring themselves of the safety of their souls at church or camp meeting. In short, as the illustrations in this chapter show, British North America in 1820 was a simple community of pioneers content to leave government to their 'betters'— the English officials and their associates.

But a scant generation later, in 1841, British North America was greatly changed. Lower Canada (now Quebec) and Upper Canada (Ontario) were joined that year by the Act of Union passed by the British Parliament to create the Province of Canada. In all the provinces, population was much increased. Montreal was becoming, for the times, a considerable little city, with good houses, shops, streets, gas lights, water supply, hotels and the other equipment of an urban community. A second French bishopric had been provided for it. Quebec, the ancient capital, was well into its second life as the lumber capital too, and its wealth was increasing on the toll of the rafts that floated down to it. Halifax, with nearly a century of time and the fortunes of war behind it, had become a provincial capital of assurance; in it the first sprouts of a local literature (remember Sam Slick, the immortal clockmaker?) were already showing. In New Brunswick, the pleasant Anglicanism of a few families in the little capital of Fredericton was to give forth men like C. G. D. Roberts, who eventually wrote an important chapter in Canadian literature.

In the Province of Canada, not only had schools been founded but colleges: King's College in Toronto; Victoria, the Methodist college, at Cobourg; Queen's, the Presbyterian, at Kingston. In Quebec, François-Xavier Garneau was writing his classic history of the country (*Histoire du Canada depuis la découverte jusqu'à nos jours*) and Laval was becoming a seat of learning sufficiently considerable to enable it in a few years (1852) to apply for and obtain a royal charter of incorporation as a university. In 1836-37, there had been built and opened the first railway in Canada —the few miles of line that connected the Richelieu River with the south shore opposite Montreal and cut a day off the journey between New York and Montreal. In Upper Canada, both the Rideau and the Welland canals had been built and work was under way on those of the St. Lawrence. Railways were constantly talked of, though in the period none of them, with the exception mentioned,

was built. In Lower Canada, the vast edifice of Notre Dame in Montreal had been completed in 1829; visible, if ugly, testimony to the strength and energy of the French race in America. In Upper Canada, Osgoode Hall had gone up in Toronto, providing space for law courts of the time. In every town and village there were newspapers. And, of course, just behind, still in very recent memory, were 'the troubles', the rebellions that in 1837-38 had torn the provinces internally apart and threatened to destroy them. The rebellions were crushed, but they succeeded all the same. By exposing the weaknesses of the old system they opened the way to self-government, eventual confederation and even the Commonwealth itself.

The old colonial system that the rebels opposed had been a haphazard growth. British colonies, it has often been asserted, had traditionally been something like Topsy— they just 'growed'. Or as the historian J. R.

LUGGAGE

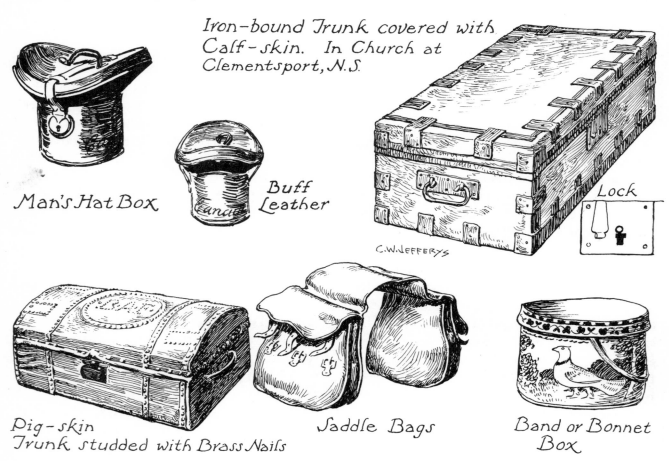

Iron-bound Trunk covered with Calf-skin. In Church at Clementsport, N.S.

Man's Hat Box

Buff Leather

Lock

C.W. JEFFERYS

Pig-skin Trunk studded with Brass Nails

Saddle Bags

Band or Bonnet Box

Cholera on board an immigration ship of the 1830s

Immigrants of the 1830s brave the backwoods

C.W.JEFFERYS

Seeley in his *Expansion of England,* was to put it, Great Britain had acquired an empire 'in fits of absence of mind'. Both assertions have some truth in them, and also a good deal of error. The first empire—the West Indian Islands and the continental colonies— was by no means all 'absence of mind', for there had been much organized effort behind it, both public and private. The results are visible, being mainly the United States. The second empire consisted of the scraps left over from the wreck of the American Revolution, though here too some modification must be made.

British North America, or what was left of it in 1783, just after the wreck, stirred no hearts. 'This last foul brat', Edmund Burke had said of Nova Scotia on its founding. 'The liberty of parading in boundless wildernesses', is the way another English publicist summed up what had been acquired by conquest from France. If anywhere in the empire the consequences of 'absence of mind' were to be found, it was surely in the British North America that was left after the American Revolution. The glory had departed, Britain's colonial sun had set; why bother about what was left? The logical thing would have been to hand them over to the new country that had emerged and wipe the slate clean.

But the colonies were kept, and the old familiar pattern began to emerge again, even though it had been proved inadequate. Loyalist migrations, Montreal fur interests, Nova Scotia and Newfoundland as supply bases for the West Indies, a pinch of national pride, and not least, jobs for the needy relations of British politicians—all such things kept the old structure going, glass all out of the windows, sky showing through the roof. No repairs of moment were necessary—or desirable. The old type of colonial administration and of trade patterns, under which the first empire had thrived to greatness, would do quite well for the second. Colonial governors came and went as before, colonial councilors gathered round them and colonial legislators met in colonial 'capitals' to bicker with them.

And all the time, there stood the former colonies, vigorously pushing westward, their progress plainly visible to the people of the provinces. They remained friends until the War of 1812 separated once and for all the people of the 'provinces' from the people of the 'states'. The war proved to be the foundation war for Upper Canada, the defence of its heritage for Lower, and for the Maritimes privateering and good times. After that war, the new wine of new provincial life was being poured into the old bottles of an ancient

Clearing the land

colonial system, and as the Good Book tells us, when that is done the old bottles are apt to break. And so it was in British North America. A generation of controversy lay ahead, a generation culminating in rebellion and a new start in 1840.

Given the system that preceded the rebellions, a new start was inevitable. Prior to the middle of the 19th century, the traditional government for British colonies was always and everywhere the same, differing from place to place only in detail. At its head was the governor, and at the governor's elbow was an appointive executive council. The Legislature consisted of two chambers, as our Parliament does today: the Legislative Council, which was appointive, comparable to our Senate, and the Legislative Assembly, which was elective, usually on a wide franchise, and was the equivalent of our House of Commons. Legislation had to passs through both houses of the legislature, receive the governor's consent and then be sent to Westminster for approval by the secretary of state for the colonies. If no approval was received back in the colony, the law in question could not go into effect. Since the Legislative Council was appointive, it invariably represented vested interests or social status, and as such more often than not found itself in conflict with the assembly. In Lower Canada, the two bodies came to polarize around race—the council was English; the assembly, French—and so an ideal basis for racial strife was provided. The only way the assembly could prevail was by refusing to pass supplies—that is, the money needed to carry on public business—thus bringing the wheels of government to a stop. In such impasses, governors were apt to dissolve the assembly and have another election, which usually brought back a house more recalcitrant than its predecessor. Unceasing strife had gone on between the assembly and the other bodies in the old colonies that became the United States, and this situation was duly transferred to the newer ones. As Chester Martin once very aptly termed it, it was 'like a fire without a chimney'.

It was in Lower Canada that smoke from this fire filled the house, with a good deal being generated in Upper Canada too, minor

The circuit rider (right), an itinerant Methodist preacher, travelling between his widely-scattered settler congregations. Below, the Royal Mail

C.W. JEFFERYS

Official fence viewers settling boundary dispute

amounts in Nova Scotia and traces in the other colonies. In Lower Canada, every problem, no matter how slight, eventually turned itself into a racial clash (as it is apt to do today), so it should not have taken much foresight to grasp what would happen sooner or later—the two people arrayed against each other and the situation so tense that bloodshed would follow. In the very first session of the first provincial legislature, 1792, there had been minor indications of the racial conflict, and as time went by there were more of them. If the province had been much better governed than it was, strife would have been moderated, though no doubt, people being what they are, the racial opposition, if it had not found one channel of expression, would have found another.

But the province was not well-governed. There was the cumbrous process of law-making already referred to and there was far too much effort from 'home' to instruct the governor in detail; in a day when letters and answers were often a matter of three or four months (and none in winter), long-range government necessarily must have been a failure. Then there were numerous appointment 'plums' to provincial offices made to lucky persons in Great Britain: colonial reformers used often to describe the empire as a vast system of charitable relief for the poor relations of the British governing classes. There was also the uncontrolled emigration of the period, on crowded, disease-ridden shipping; thousands of people dumped into the port of Quebec, often to depend on the charity of the inhabitants and occasionally to spread disease far and wide. In 1832, the cholera, having finished off many of the emigrants en route, pursued the rest of them on up the river, to Montreal, to Kingston, to York, and even as far as Detroit, mowing down many of the native-born in the process.

But chiefly, perhaps, there was the land granting system. In any new country the land is the obvious form of obtainable wealth

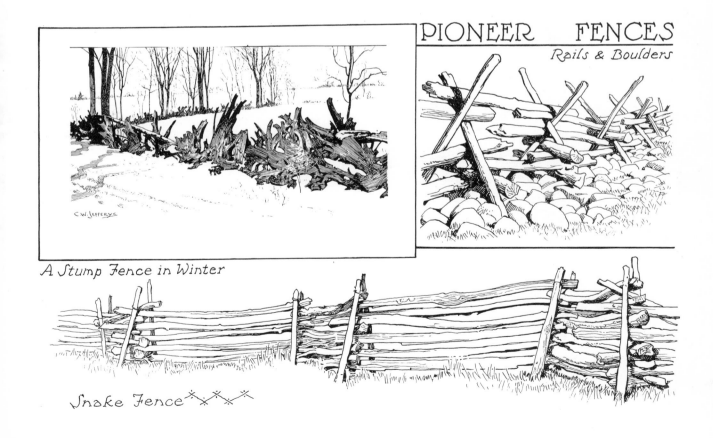

PIONEER FENCES
Rails & Boulders

A Stump Fence in Winter

Snake Fence

C.W. JEFFERYS

Boiling wood-ash for potash to make soap

34

and anyone who has any kind of inside track invariably does his best to acquire as much of it as he can, not for personal use, but to sell to later arrivals. Land-speculating has been the major form of sport in every new country from the day Columbus made his landfall down to the present. In British North America the game was played with pertinacity and success. A concrete example or two will illustrate what went on. One W. B. Felton came to Lower Canada in 1815, apparently with considerable capital. He received a grant of 2,000 acres in the Eastern Townships and his family another 2,000. In the course of the next 18 years, Felton made innumerable applications for further grants and while the authorities in England were always worried and sometimes hostile about these, somehow or other the grants were forthcoming. So were children, until the score stood at nine. Felton managed to get 9,400 acres in their names, in addition to 14,141 for himself. His case was defended on the ground that he had opened roads and built mills. But all this land was given free! A similar case was that of the original William Price, who in his own name

Threshing grain with swivelled flails

C. W. JEFFERYS

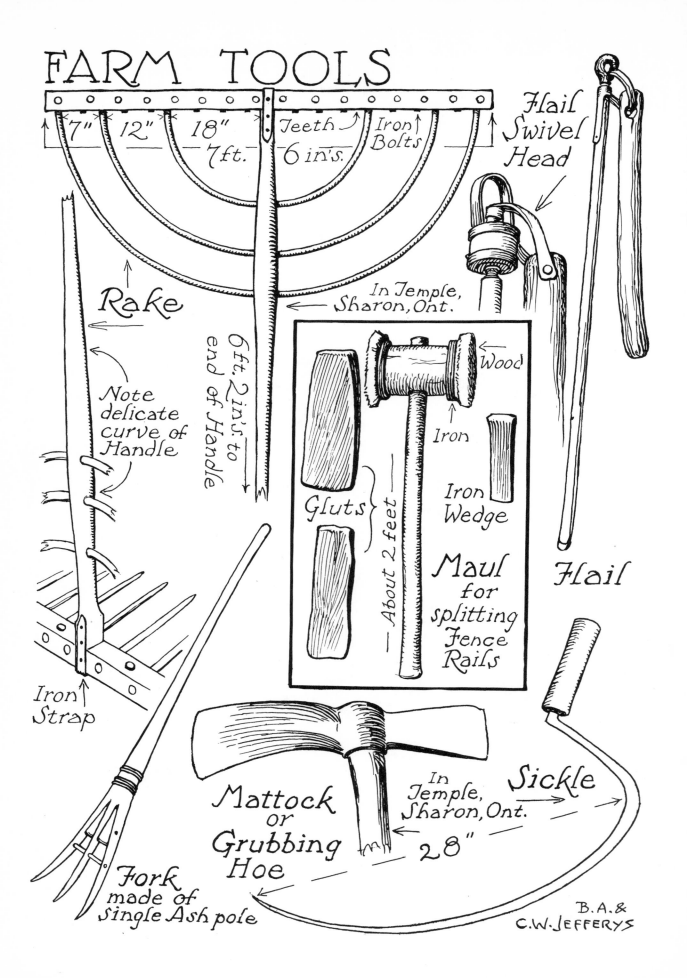

FARM TOOLS

7"   12"   18"   Teeth   Iron Bolts
7ft.   6 in's.

Rake

Note delicate curve of Handle

6 ft. 2 in's. to end of Handle

Iron Strap

Flail Swivel Head

In Temple, Sharon, Ont.

Wood

Iron

Iron Wedge

Gluts

About 2 feet

Maul for splitting Fence Rails

Flail

Mattock or Grubbing Hoe

In Temple, Sharon, Ont.

Sickle

28"

Fork made of single Ash pole

B.A. & C.W.JEFFERYS

and that of his 'associates' received a whole township. The 'township associate' system was well understood: it usually involved collecting a couple of hundred names on a petition for a township and then paying each signatory a small sum for his signature and the abandonment of his claim. Collective land grants of this sort led to litigation, as heir succeeded heir, which extended over generations. The eagle eyes of French members of the assembly naturally quickly spotted what was going on, and translated it into a looting of their inheritance by *les Anglais*.

All such grievances, and many more, were set down in the famous Ninety-Two Resolutions of 1834, whose submission to the legislature was one of the stages on the road to rebellion. The 92 resolutions comprised a complete bill of complaints; too complete, for they included trivialities. It is interesting to find among them a complaint included in French indictments of the English down to this day about the virtual monopoly of *postes* by *les Anglais*. A *poste*, a government job with security and status, has always

meant much to a people conscious of status and insecure economically.

When favoritism was linked to race, language, religion, and leadership, strife was inevitable. In Louis-Joseph Papineau the aggrieved French found a leader. He was born to politics, his father having been an assemblyman before him. He became a lawyer and throve sufficiently well to acquire a seigneury at Montebello up the Ottawa River. His father had been a land surveyor and as such something of a radical, for surveyors in French Canada, largely self-taught at that period, were men on the way up, men who had to push aside the favorites of fortune. Wilfrid Laurier's father was also a surveyor. Louis-Joseph lost his Catholic faith while at college in Quebec and although he respected it, he never regained it. He soon discovered that he was an orator, and as an orator, he was to gain remarkable ascendance over a people always under the spell of the spoken word. His attitude, his complaints and his motives can be easily understood, for they were exactly the same as those of every

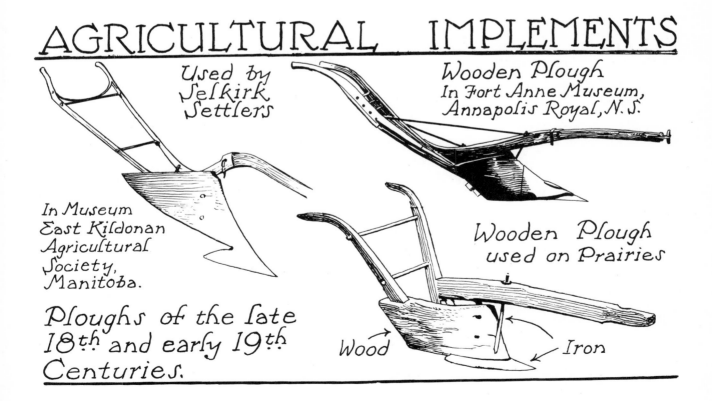

AGRICULTURAL IMPLEMENTS

Used by Selkirk Settlers

Wooden Plough In Fort Anne Museum, Annapolis Royal, N.S.

In Museum East Kildonan Agricultural Society, Manitoba.

Wooden Plough used on Prairies

Ploughs of the late 18th and early 19th Centuries.

Wood   Iron

SHINGLE MAKING

K 21"
Maul for striking Frow

12"
Frow

Splitting block with Frow

other left-wing French-speaking Canadian who has ever existed. English-Canadians are constantly asking what Quebec wants. The question is so simple (to the historian at least) that it appears naive. Quebec wants what *la race française en Amérique* has wanted from the day of Lévis's surrender outside Montreal in 1760; she wants to reverse the Conquest, that is all. So that whatever the terms of the day may be, the situation never changes: reverse the Conquest, 'get the English off our necks', and if possible out of the house. People who cannot understand the psychology of a conquered people can never get very far in Canadian history and affairs.

Papineau's line very quickly became that of making the most of every grievance. The colonial authorities obligingly provided him with enough. They could have appointed

him to the Executive Council and offered him an important *poste* and there was a period when he might have accepted. But the matter was 'referred home' and referred back again and back again, until some years had elapsed. When an offer finally was made, it came too late and Papineau's pride refused to let him become a councilor. He remained in perpetual opposition and as a rule he was able to carry with him his fellow 'Canadians' (no English-speaking person used that term in those days).

In 1822 a neat little scheme was got up among the Montreal merchants to unite the two provinces. Upper Canada, whose population was smaller than that of Lower, would be given equal representation in the assembly and English made the sole official language. This was sounding the tocsin indeed. Papineau hastened over to England and managed to get the proposed Union Bill indefinitely postponed. Like many another French-speaking Canadian, he was at home in England and he had a clearer and more scholarly idea of the nature of the English constitution than had most of the mere businessmen of Montreal. That constituted another element of strain—the difference in cultural level between the two groups which was in favor of the French.

The course of politics in Lower Canada during the 1820s and early 1830s bears considerable resemblance to the course of the parliamentary struggle in England against Charles I during the 1630s, and men like Papineau were aware of the parallelism. 'The Tribune of the People', as Papineau came to be dubbed, was consciously waging war against 'the great', that is, against office holders and rich *Anglais,* and against 'the king' in the person of the governor. His weapon was mainly, 'the power of the purse':

once the executive had spent the revenues coming directly to it from such sources as the proceeds of land sales and timber rights, it had to come to the assembly to ask for a vote of taxation. This gave the assembly much bargaining power, though the Crown revenues were too great to give it complete control. The assembly used its taxing power to get other measures past by adopting a device from English experience known as 'tacking'. This involved 'tacking on' to a revenue bill a measure unrelated to it, one that council or governor had previously refused to accept.

The pot of discord kept boiling merrily all through the 1820s. In 1828 there was a full dress parliamentary inquiry in England into the affairs of Lower Canada, but no one over there seems to have understood the real nature of the situation and so the result was a mere palliative in the form of the offer to surrender Crown revenues in return for a permanent civil list, that is, salaries guaranteed indefinitely for a given number of major

← 12 inches →

Draw Knife

Tapering Shingles with Draw Knife on Shaving Horse

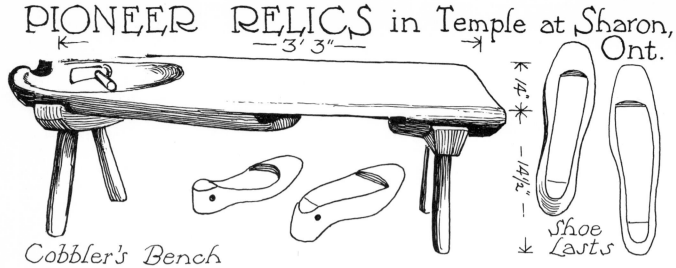

PIONEER RELICS in Temple at Sharon, Ont.

—3′ 3″—

14″

14½″

Cobbler's Bench

Shoe Lasts

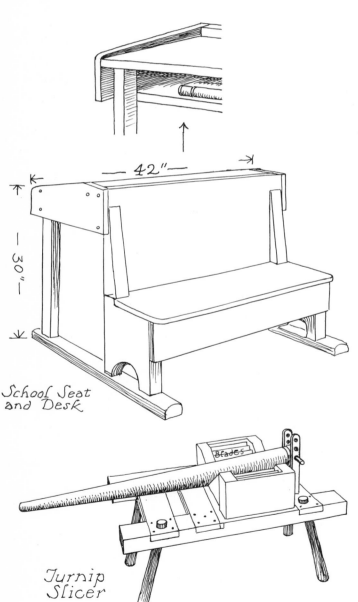

42″

30″

School Seat and Desk

Blades

Turnip Slicer

officials. This offer was not accepted, nor were later ones suggesting smaller and smaller civil lists.

The only constructive measure advanced by Papineau's party was to make the Legislative Council elective. This measure, which had American example to support it, meant a large French majority in the council: the English would have lost one of their major citadels of power and a combined legislature would have been able to bring much greater pressure on the government. The proposal had no chance of acceptance.

Discord began to mount in the 1830s. There was a riot in Montreal in which troops fired on the crowd and two or three citizens of French origin were killed: the parallel to the Boston 'Massacre' of 1770, in which under similar circumstances four or five Yankees were killed by the bullets of the redcoats, was at once drawn. Then doubts arose as to the good faith of one or two of the governors, especially Lord Gosford, ironically a man of untarnished honor. All this was accompanied by heady speeches within the assembly and without: the fine art of rabble rousing is not new. In reply, the English began to form semi-military organizations thinly disguised as constitutional associations. Papineau staged a series of open-air

A water-powered grist mill

LAMPS, CANDLESTICKS and LANTERNS

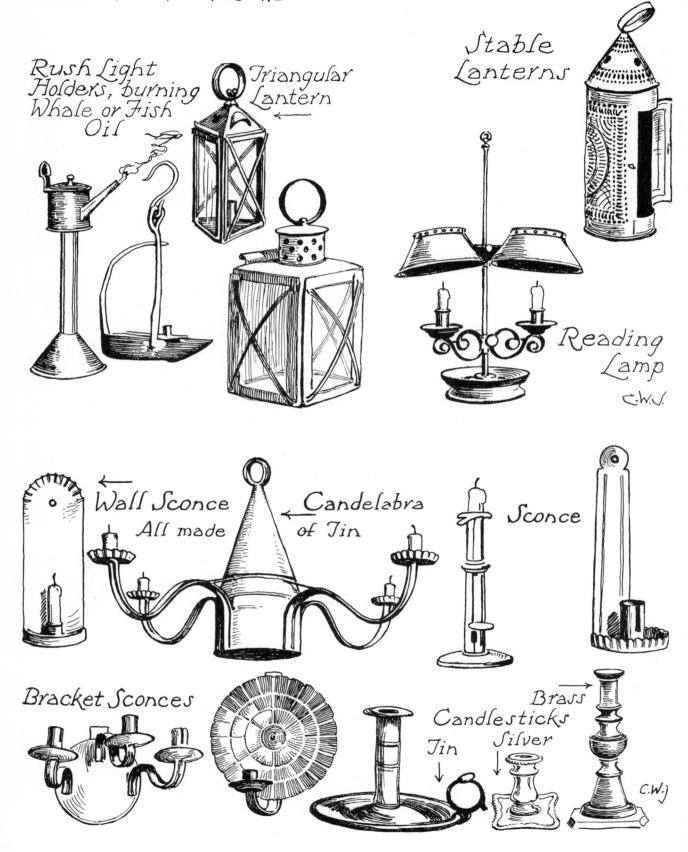

Rush Light Holders, burning Whale or Fish Oil

Triangular Lantern

Stable Lanterns

Reading Lamp

C.W.J.

Wall Sconce All made

Candelabra of Tin

Sconce

Bracket Sconces

Brass Candlesticks Silver

Tin

C.W.J.

mass meetings, at which his eloquence whipped the crowds to fever heat. Secret drilling began. The end was clearly in sight.

In December, 1837, fighting broke out. Here again, there was a parallel in history, for Sir John Colborne, the British commander, sent out a force to the southward of Montreal, much as Gage had sent his men out from Boston to Concord in 1775. The troops were fired on, and the first of the little battles of the rebellion took place. The French-Canadians of the countryside—with some English leaders among them—gave a fair account of themselves, but there the parallel with the American Revolution ended. There was no Bunker Hill, only the defeat at St. Eustache, not because of any lack of fighting spirit among the people of the Montreal-Richelieu district, but because of lack of preparation and of divided leadership. When, in the summer of 1837, Papineau had begun to see where his path was leading, he tried to retrace it and had advised against non-constitutional measures. It had been too late. When fighting broke out, he fled across the border. The rebels were crushed, many of them imprisoned and a number of them executed.

Surprisingly the rebellion did not turn into a long guerilla war, such as occurred off and on in Ireland for centuries, and there were two main reasons. First, disaffection had manifested itself only in the Montreal-Richelieu area, not at Quebec, and secondly, the rebels lacked the support of the church. Many of the local *curés* probably were sympathetic but the constituted authorities of the church were not: they came down, as Catholic authority always must, on the side of 'the powers that be which are ordained of God'. Why not? church leaders would have asked at the time. What was to be gained by rebellion against the armed might of Britain? Most likely absorption into the English and Protestant American union. And was not Papineau a free thinker? Why follow him?

LIGHTING ACCESSORIES

Candle Box

Candle Snuffers

Wheel Tinder Box

Candlestick Tinder Box

Flint & Steel

Candle Mould

C.W.J.

A general store, about 1820

In the same year and the same month, December, 1837, rebellion broke out in Upper Canada. It might seem as if the two were a concerted movement, but this is not the case. Papineau and Mackenzie had some correspondence, that is all. A rebellion did occur, however, in Upper Canada, and its effects were far-reaching. It is therefore necessary to look at things in the upper province in order to get an explanation for it.

Upper Canada in the early 19th century was only one place of the many in which people of English speech and the Protestant religion were making a vigorous attack on the bush: the same thing was going on at a score of points in the United States, as well as beyond the seas in Australia and South Africa. Essentially the same conditions existed in all these new settlements, and to a considerable extent the same grievances: favoritism at the little local capital, difficulties of communication, unfair and often corrupt land

grants, uncertainty of the title to land (and what could make a man more uneasy than to have doubts that the home he was painfully making might not really be his own). If Upper Canada had its special struggle over the Clergy Reserves, (the awkward one-seventh of all its land that was reserved for the support of 'a Protestant clergy'), New South Wales in Australia had its objections to the policy called 'transportation', which made the country a dumping-ground for convicts, so no claim to being unique can be established on such grounds. It may have been that there were more grievances in Upper Canada than elsewhere, it may have been that there were many Americans in its population not accustomed to taking grievances quietly or it may have been that there happened to be a few prominent trouble-makers present in Upper Canada; whatever the exact explanation, discontent began to bubble in Upper Canada soon after the turn of the century. It died

A village dance in 1840

HEATING STOVES

1843

Cathedral Type 1845

down during the war of 1812, then resumed again, to go on slowly mounting during the 1820s, have its pace accelerated during the 1830s and at last, as in Lower Canada, to break out in rebellion. The course of events in the two provinces thus ran parallel.

In Upper Canada difficulties more or less peculiar to the region probably would not have caused rebellion in themselves, but they provided some of the material from which rebellion arises. Among them the Clergy Reserves have been mentioned: they kept awkward areas out of settlement but, more provokingly, they were constant and visible symbols of denominational discrimination. If the hardy pioneering people of Upper Canada cherished one sentiment more than any other, it surely was that they were as good as any man. No pulling of forelocks to the lord of the manor in Upper Canada, none of the semi-feudalism, such as the annual rent payment to the seigneur known as *les ceus-et-rentes*, that existed in Lower Canada and that was supportable to a people brought up under authority.

Add to Clergy Reserves the marriage question. Why should Anglican clergy alone have the inherent right to perform the marriage ceremony? Anglicans were not even a majority in the province. The Clergy Reserves and the marriage question cooled the ardor of many a frontier Methodist and Baptist—and of many who were not frontier. Among these was Egerton Ryerson, son of a Loyalist and of unimpeachable loyalty himself. As a young man in 1825 he took on the Anglican champion, Archdeacon Strachan of York, and a pamphlet war ensued of which Ryerson had rather the better. Thenceforward, the Methodists, whose loyalty suffered another indignity in being often impugned because of their associations with their fellow Methodist organizations south of the border, became a power to be reckoned with in Upper Canada politics.

Still another factor in denominational dispute was the question of a local college. Strachan was determined that if one were to be established, it would be under the control of his church; that is, of himself. Much to the annoyance of other denominations, he persisted in regarding the Church of England as the official, if not exactly the established church in the colony. His efforts to maintain control of the new institution, King's College, prevented an effective college from being established, thus delaying the cause of higher education in the provincial capital for 15 years and more, and incidentally giving rise to two other colleges in other parts of the province: Victoria at Cobourg and Queen's at Kingston.

One quite exceptional family cannot be passed over in even the briefest account of Upper Canada at the period: the Baldwins. William Warren Baldwin had come from southern Ireland to Upper Canada in 1790. He belonged to a class of immigrant that was to become not uncommon in Upper Canada, the 'small gentry', many of them Irish Protestants. He had grown up in an Ireland in

which Protestants, thanks to the pressures of the American Revolution, had squeezed out of the British government a considerable measure of self-government, under their own Parliament. His experiences came to Canada along with himself and they were duly passed on to his Canadian-born son, Robert. The Baldwins, father and son, came to see that the road to content in a colonial government was that which had been partially followed in Ireland, namely, more and more self-government. The device that would crown the structure of self-government was also plain to them: require the governor, through the leading officers of the Crown in the colony, to get his measures approved by the Legislative Assembly. It sounds simple and obvious today; in those days it was almost revolutionary, for it proposed the submission of the governor, the king's representative, to the elected assembly. William Warren

MORE STOVES

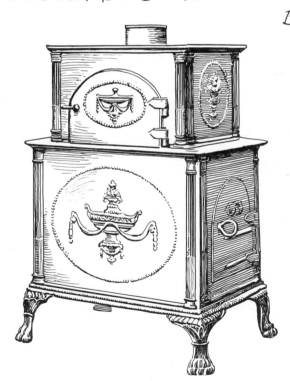

Box Stove
made at St. Maurice Forges,
Quebec. Early 19th Century.

Baltimore Cook Stove

Box Stove
made at
Normandale
Furnace
Norfolk County
Ont., about
1820.

47

FOUR–POSTER BEDS, CRADLES and WARMING PAN.

Observe side curtains

Mahogany Bed. Posts carved in "fern-leaf" or "feather" pattern.

Beside the Bed are Steps by which to climb into it.

Hinged Lid

BED ROOM FURNITURE

Wash hand Stand

Baldwin submitted this scheme to the Duke of Wellington in 1828, not long before the latter went out of office as Prime Minister. In the following decade, as tension mounted, his son proposed it to the governor of the day, Sir Francis Bond Head, only to have the governor accept the proposals in a form so limited as to ensure their failure. Gradually Baldwin's phrase for it took hold and became a constitutional rallying cry—Responsible Government. With the achievement later on, in 1848, of Responsible Government, Baldwin (together with his friend and partner from Lower Canada, Louis-Hippolyte Lafontaine) brought self-government to Canada.

Robert Baldwin walked a dangerous road in the 1830s, for tempers were so high that he might easily have been lumped in with the extremists and accused of disloyalty. His was a paradoxical family: all its associations were with the Tory right; the Baldwins were Anglicans, large landowners, 'gentry'. Their friends and relatives were all in the same camp. Yet they persisted in their role of con-

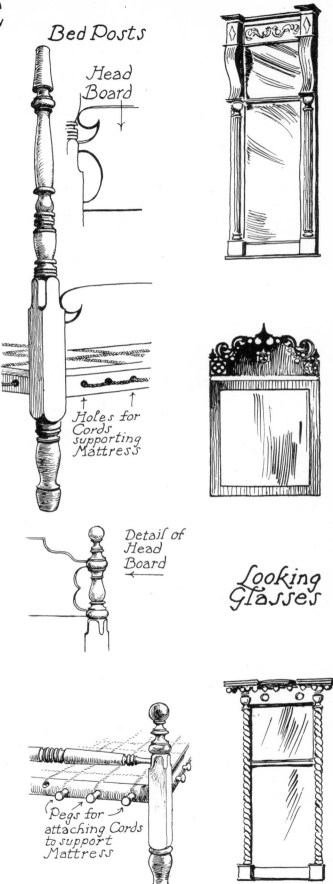

Bed Posts

Head Board

Holes for Cords supporting Mattress

Detail of Head Board

Looking Glasses

Pegs for attaching Cords to support Mattress

stitutional reformers, came through the rebellion unscathed and Robert lived to see the triumph of the family conception, that Irish import, Responsible Government.

There were men in the colony who were neither as wise nor as firmly in the middle of the road as the Baldwins. Of these, one name at once leaps to everyone's lips, William Lyon Mackenzie. But Mackenzie was not the only man who made himself obnoxious to the 'family compact' clique. There had been Robert Gourlay, whom the clique had succeeded in harrying out of the land. There were others less provocative, such as the Bidwells. Gourlay and Mackenzie would have been restless and uneasy members of any society: in Upper Canada, privilege and favoritism that came close to corruption were so rampant that the natural tendencies of these two men were enhanced. Mackenzie found magnificent material in such a situation for his newspaper and he became the province's first political journalist. By the 1830s, he had uncovered a dozen unsavory situations and was making appeal enough to the public to get himself elected both as mayor of York and member of the assembly. The device resorted to by his enemies to subdue him— votes for his expulsion from the assembly (followed by re-election, followed by expulsion, followed by re-election) made him a popular hero. It became clear to him that until a change in the nature of government was made, little reform could be accomplished. The failure of the Head-Baldwin experiment in 1836 apparently convinced him that things had got beyond debate. No more than Papineau did Mackenzie deliberately and decisively think of rebellion. Both of them were 'rhetoricians intoxicated with their own verbosity' and they talked themselves out on a limb from which they could not crawl back and so had to jump off. In Upper Canada, no sane man who had coolly calculated means, ends and risks would have resorted to arms in 1837. Rebellion, to be successful, requires the sympathy of most of the people, requires careful preparation, gathering of arms, drilling, plans for the en-

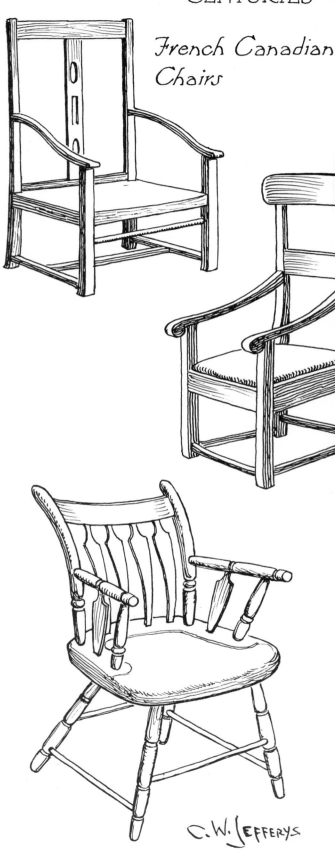

CHAIRS 18TH & EARLY 19TH CENTURIES

French Canadian Chairs

C. W. JEFFERYS

suing government. The only factor that Mackenzie was justified in interpreting in favor of success was Bond Head's foolhardiness in sending most of the troops off to help out in Lower Canada, but when a faction is in quite a small minority, the absence of troops is not enough.

Mackenzie's rebellion, as an armed revolt, was a flash in a pan: a few shots (the pleasant legend is that these were quite enough to frighten both sides into taking to their heels) and it was all over. Mackenzie was a fugitive and some of the ringleaders were under arrest. The measures of repression that followed had an unpleasant atmosphere of vindictiveness about them: they widened the split in Upper Canadian society. Thousands of good settlers got out. Public credit was undermined. The great works that had been going forward on the St. Lawrence canals came to a standstill. The future, in a province given over to reaction, looked dark. Matters were not helped

when the new governor turned out to have been the man who, as Governor of Tasmania, had spent the previous few years building those vast and melancholy structures still to be seen not far from Hobart and destined in their day to be the unhappy abiding places of the convicts. A master of convicts for a province of free men? The prospect was not pleasant.

While neither rebellion was formidable as a rising in arms their results were of basic importance and they have influenced life in Canada down to our own days. The rebellion in Lower Canada could easily be interpreted as that of a conquered people against their conquerors—naturally, their tyrannical conquerors—and in this way it was interpreted by most people of French speech. Yet as has been made clear, the church had been against rebellion and those who took up arms had

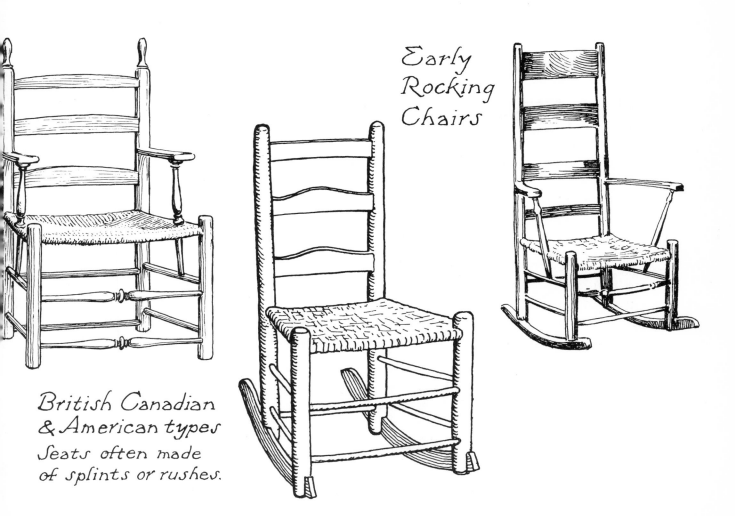

Early Rocking Chairs

British Canadian & American types Seats often made of splints or rushes.

51

UPPER CANADA DOORWAYS

Prest House, Queenston

On Dundas Road

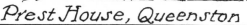

From Photos in "The Early Architecture of Ontario" by Prof. E.R. Arthur

Near Prescott

At Grimsby

Locust Hall St. David's

been drawn almost solely from the Montreal-Richelieu district. While the rebels had the sympathy of their compatriots, few French-Canadians could find wisdom in the course they had taken. A province historically conservative to a degree that would have made even a family compact Tory shudder could hardly look with equanimity on armed rebellion against 'the powers that be'.

In Upper Canada, the interpretation of the rebellion was simple: bad government. Remedy that, and there would be few who would wish to depart from their traditional allegiance.

Luckily, for once in history the hour and the man coincided. The Imperial government decided to send out still another commission of investigation, and also a new Governor-in-Chief. This was Lord Durham, Radical Jack, as he had been called for his leading part in securing the passage of the Great Reform Bill of 1832. A peculiar choice for colonies in rebellion? Yes, but a peculiar man

had chosen him, Lord Melbourne, the Whig Prime Minister. Durham was restless, difficult, brilliant. Melbourne had first got him out of the country by sending him off as Ambassador at St. Petersburg, and now this further chance presented itself to send him even farther away. So Durham duly came to Canada. He brought with him as able and unorthodox a group of assistants and disciples as must ever have accompanied a British pro-consul abroad, men nearly all of whom entertained advanced ideas on colonies and had minds as sharp as their ideas were advanced. None could have been more in contrast with the procession of grave and stolid generals that had preceded them.

The result of all this was five months of hard work, marked by a final temperamental explosion by Durham in the last month or so, a public proclamation by him which might almost have been interpreted as advice to start fighting again, and the great man's resignation. There followed another spate of

WROUGHT IRONWORK

Door Latches

Spikes with Angular & Round Hammered Heads

Square-headed Nail Section

Typical Iron-barred Window of Quebec

hard work on board ship on the way back to England, a month or so there and then the appearance, less than three months after the mission had left Canada, of the great, long and to-be-famous *Report* of 1839, brilliantly and hastily conceived, as brilliantly, hastily and soundly written, 'the greatest state paper of the 19th century' as it sometimes has been called. If anyone wishes to understand the Lower Canada of the 1830s—that is, the Quebec of today—all he need do is read the Durham *Report*. It is readily available. It put its finger at once on the trouble in Lower Canada. 'I expected to find a contest between a government and a people: I found two nations warring in the bosom of a single state: I found a struggle, not of principles, but of races,' wrote Durham.

On Upper Canada, Durham had relatively little to say. He spent only a short time in the province, but had one significant interview—with Robert Baldwin. Baldwin evi-dently sold him on Responsible Government, for here was the central recommendation of the Report:

'It needs but to follow out consistently the principles of the British constitution and introduce into the government of these great colonies those wise provisions by which alone the workings of the representative system can in any country be rendered harmonious and efficient . . . I would not impair a single prerogative of the Crown . . . But the Crown must . . . submit to the necessary consequences of representative institutions; and if it has to carry on the government in unison with a representative body, it must consent to carry it on by means of those in whom that representative body has confidence . . . Every purpose of popular control might be combined with every advantage of vesting the immediate choice of advisers in the Crown, were the colonial governor to be instructed to secure the cooperation of the

YORK BOATS

Polling up a shallow river

Under Sail

Courtesy of Hudson's Bay Co.

C.W. Jefferys

VESSELS of the GREAT LAKES

A bluff-bowed Schooner

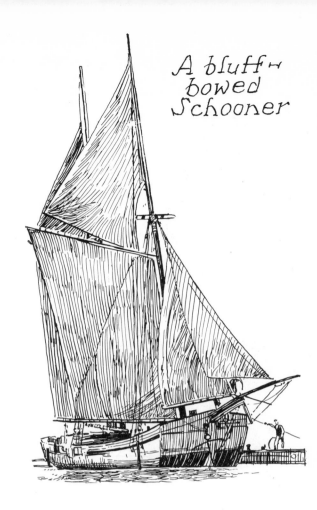

A Stonehooker

A Barquentine

C·W·J·

CARIOLES and SLEIGHS

About 1800

Cariole, about 1815

Officer's Sleigh 1826

At Fredericton 1835

Habitant's Wood Sleigh

About 1850

After Old Prints

From Krieghoff 1854

56

assembly in his policy by entrusting its administration to such men as could command a majority . . .'

In Great Britain, there was opposition to adopting the principle Durham outlined. The Colonial Secretary of the day, Lord John Russell, thought it would be impossible to give such a measure of power to a colonial assembly and have it remain colonial. It took several strong and able letters from Joseph Howe of Nova Scotia to argue him down. Howe had encountered in Nova Scotia the same general conditions that existed in the Canadas, but not in so extreme a measure. He was more of a statesman than either Mackenzie or Papineau and consequently while there was much discontent in Nova Scotia, there was no suggestion of an appeal to arms. That province actually led the way to Responsible Government in British North America, which was accorded it in 1846.

Unfortunately Durham's sound view on Responsible Government was not accompanied by equal penetration into the nature of French Canada. What he had to propose in respect to it was simply that the sooner the French became English, the better for all concerned. This has never increased his popularity in French Canada!

Had it not been for the rebellions, discontent would have slumbered on, makeshifts would have been resorted to and it is hard to see what alternative course history would have taken. It is quite possible that a solution to the great conundrum—how to remain a colony and yet be independent—would not have got an answer at all. It is therefore not too much to assert that by providing the solution—Responsible Government—the Canadas (and especially Robert Baldwin) opened the gate for the modern Commonwealth, which is no small accomplishment.

The colonies differed so from each other that the solution of the political difficulties of one did not imply success when the same devices were applied to another. Constitu-

EARLY BRIDGES

Corduroy Pole Bridge

G.W. JEFFERYS

Square Log Bridge
Detail of Pier
From Bouchette

Stone Pier Bridge

57

tional and political reform consequently took different shape in all of them. In Newfoundland, the economy was so precarious that no sound basis could be found for self-government. The leaders of the ordinary men fought the snugly-ensconced office-holders and merchants, and this class struggle coincided with the racial and religious cleavage between Irish Roman Catholics and Anglican Englishmen. Two civil wars at once, even if fought only with shillelaghs, are rather too much for self-government, which in consequence was modified in the 1830s into government by appointed governor, with an assembly partially appointed, partially elective.

In Prince Edward Island, the issue was also economic; whether absentee proprietors should maintain their ownership of the soil or whether the land should be put into the hands of ordinary small farmers. Year after year nothing had been done and parts of the island were described in the 1830s as almost in a state of civil strife, with burly 'squatters' standing off owners' agents and attempting to maintain their *de facto* possession. The problem was not solved in the period, but remained one of the grievances which it eventually required Confederation (1873) to liquidate.

Proud New Brunswickers sometimes insist that it was their province that led the way in reform. They claim that in the early 1830s, the assembly, through some of its leaders, broke the hold that a small, tight knot of 'family compact' men headed by the Surveyor General, Thomas Baillie, had on the good places and especially on the revenues from the public lands of the province. As a result, the assembly secured control of what were termed 'the casual and territorial revenues of the Crown'—which because of

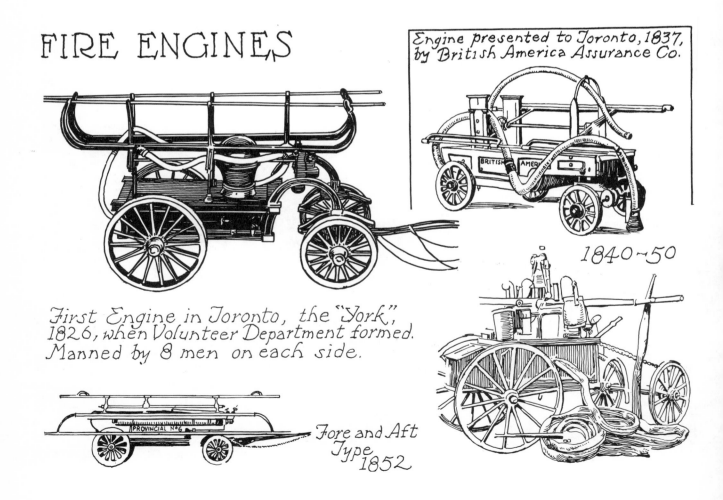

FIRE ENGINES

Engine presented to Toronto, 1837, by British America Assurance Co.

1840~50

First Engine in Toronto, the "York", 1826, when Volunteer Department formed. Manned by 8 men on each side.

Fore and Aft Type 1852

The FIRST LOCOMOTIVES

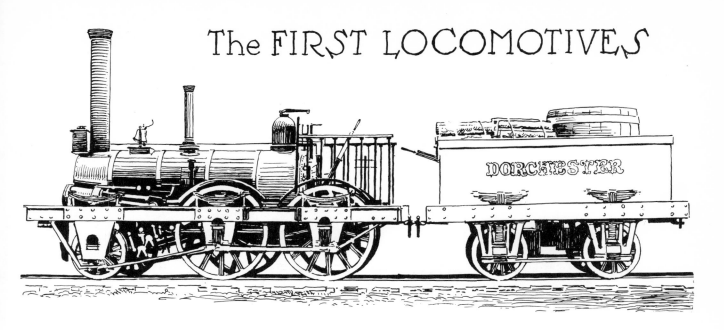

The "Sampson"
First Locomotive in Maritime Provinces Built in England. In 1837, ran from Stellarton Coal Mines to Pictou Harbour
Now in front of Nova Scotian Hotel, Halifax

The "Dorchester"
First Locomotive in Lower Canada, on LaPrarie Railway 1836
Model reconstructed by Canadian National Railways for the centenary

Political meeting 1837

Rebels march down Yonge Street to attack Toronto, 1837

the sale of timber lands were large—and its leaders got places in the executive council. Thenceforth there was harmony between governor, council and assembly, which, in the understanding of the time and place, was Responsible Government. There is a serious qualification to be imposed on this, however, for the assembly itself was in the control of the timber operators (many of them of old Loyalist families). What had happened seems to have been that in 1833 a very small family group at the top—the Odell-Baillie connection—had had to yield to a larger but by no means all-embracing group farther down. New Brunswick as a result of the fight against Baillie did not become a democracy but a somewhat more widespread oligarchy.

The political evolution in Nova Scotia has always attracted interest because of the man at its centre, the magnetic, eloquent Joe Howe. A young man when he became caught up in public life, Howe, in defending himself in a famous libel suit, not only won his case but made the first breach in the ramparts of Nova Scotia family compactism. For years the province had been in the hands of a nice, snug little group in Halifax, five of them members of one firm, nearly all of them Anglicans, most of them with extremely well-paid public positions. In their corporate capacity, they formed both the Executive and Legislative Councils (which were not distinguished the one from the other) and they met in private. When Howe let daylight into this cosy nest, the Colonial Office separated Executive and Legislative Councils and made it clear that Executive Councilors would somehow or other have to have the confidence of the assembly. It took nearly six years more, however, before the transition was effected. Even so, Nova Scotia was the first colony to be officially granted Responsible Government, in 1846. Its pioneering role was mainly played by Joseph Howe. Howe's celebrated *Four Letters Addressed to Lord John Russell, Colonial Secretary*, in 1839 provided public documents fully entitled to rank alongside Durham's *Report* in their telling literary style, the clarity and the cogency of their arguments.

It is clear that by the late 1830s something had to be done. All the colonies were growing in population. New Brunswick was building dozens of ships every year, Nova Scotians were to be found on every ocean.

Inland, the trees were falling fast, new fields appearing, new villages, new towns. Everywhere there was vigorous local life. Every colony wished progressive reform, none wanted change in allegiance. Because they divided men into groups, some clinging to things as they were or to their own privileges, others looking to necessary change, the rebellions provided the necessary foundation on which to build: here lay the basis of the party system that has come down to our own days. In general terms, if you are a Liberal (still more a New Democrat) in 1967, the chances are that you would have looked with a certain degree of sympathy on the rebels of 1837. The events of 1837 and the succeeding years therefore sum up British American history to that period and open the door through which the future could be dimly discerned. For the Canadas, the Act of Union duly followed in 1840 and in that decade Responsible Government for all the major colonies.

Battle of St. Eustache, 1837

"1837"

C.W JEFFERYS

Rebels drilling in North York, 1837

Young Joseph Howe electioneers in Halifax

Confederation

by HARRY BRUCE, *from P. B. Waite's*
The Life and Times of Confederation

Champagne launching for the ship of state

On September 15th, 1864, in the dusty, shady village of Charlottetown (population 7,000), a newspaper called *Ross's Weekly* unloaded on its readers the following indignant and curiously lip-licking account of a certain social event that had occurred in town:

'A few days after the close of the circus, a great public 'Ball and Supper' is announced; the evening of the day arrives; the proud and the gay, arrayed in fashion's gauds, flock to the scene where revelry presides . . . Pleasure panoplied in lustful smiles meets and embraces exuberant Joy . . . the fascinating dance goes merrily, and the libidinous waltz with its lascivious entwinements whiles in growing excitement; the swelling bosom and the voluptuous eye tell the story of intemperate revel . . . In this scene, where intrigue schemes sin . . . our moralist mingles; here he rocks his piety to sleep, and cradles his morality in forgiveness; and the saint who could not tolerate satan in the circus, embraces the Prince of Darkness in the gilded scene of fashion's vices, and the reeking slough of debauchery.'

Now the saint, our moralist, the victim of all this eloquent invective was the Charlottetown *Protestant*, a newspaper that had just finished attacking Slaymaker and Nichols' Olympic Circus for fleecing the public. *Ross's Weekly* happened to *like* the circus and, anyway, John Ross generally resented the snooty way the *Protestant* expressed itself. Moreover,

his paper, like many of the other 380-odd noisy little newspapers that served British North America, was volatile, testy, and highly personal. Therefore, the fact that Ross should print such an *exposé* was not surprising.

What *was* surprising about it—and the thing that makes it intriguing even now, even 103 years later—was that the guest list in that reeking slough of debauchery, the gentlemen who were helping Pleasure panoplied in lustful smiles meet and embrace exuberant Joy, the very libidinous waltzers and intemperate revellers themselves, included virtually all the solemn-looking citizens whom we now revere as The Fathers of Confederation.

Yes, those same stiff-necked characters in the famous group portrait . . . those fellows with the mutton-chop whiskers and the dark, heavy, discreet, narrow-legged woollen suits . . . with their cheeks full of potatoes and their apparently glum, Victorian, Sunday-morning faces . . . those same men, the whole rollicking bunch of them, they stayed up all through the night of September 7-8, 1864, at this Grand Ball at Province House in Charlottetown.

They arrived at 10, and they danced the local women around the hall, and they boozed it up, and they made florid speeches, and they didn't even start to eat till one in the morning. Then, somewhere around 5 a.m., they all made their way down through the warm island fog to the harbor and climbed aboard the steamship *Queen Victoria* for a trip to Nova Scotia.

There they would continue their 'deliberations'. They were founding a nation, and all through that astonishing, euphoric and frequently comic summer and autumn of 1864 they were proving that man does not found nations on bread alone.

By 1865, the Saint John *Weekly Telegraph* was crudely describing the historic Charlottetown and Quebec conferences as 'the great intercolonial drunk of last year'. The *Perth Courier* referred to Confederation as 'the measure of the Quebec ball-room and the oyster-supper statesmen', and, even while the Quebec Conference was still underway, the *Berliner Journal* was so bold as to suggest that no matter what the delegates did on their forthcoming trip to Canada West they could not possibly expect any worse hangovers than they'd already acquired. *Barney Rooney's Letters,* a satiric column in the *Halifax Citizen* mercilessly derided the Fathers for their conference-table habits:

'John A. '. . . but hand us the tipple iv ye iver stop suppin' to see iv it's strong enough; and toss a lemon to Tilley, the sowl, iv he must do penance like a patriarch.'

'I'll hae whuskey,' sez Jarge (Brown) . . . 'My certie, ye're richt though, Darcie lad, aboot the danger o' gangin' ower early tae the polls . . . Dinna ye think sae, Mister Crupper?'

'Sir,' sez Tupper, as he dried the bottom iv his tumbler, and held it handy to D'Arcy's ladle, 'the well understood wishes iv the people are so notoriously in favor iv this scheme that it would be a reckless and infamous policy to put them to the trouble of expressing themselves . . .'

'. . . the whole set staggered on to the Confrince omnibus, in the top of good humour, Brown droning out 'Soggarth Aroon' to plaze D'Arcy, and D'Arcy blarneying the Scotch to plase Brown, and McCully and Tupper swearin' etarnal friendship on Confederashun . . .'

It is clear then that there was far more to the founding of Canada than the old group portrait betrays. There was far more than the school textbooks care to reveal, far more warmth, passion, intemperance and color than we are used to associating with 19th century Canada.

The thing we forget, in our more solemn tributes to the Fathers of Confederation, is that they were men who cared violently about their politics; that they were at the seething heart of a whole society of businessmen, churchmen, farmers, bigots, factions, fanatical regionalists, goons, quacks, eccentrics, and brilliantly vicious newspapers; and that all these people and forces cared violently about *their* politics, too. Reports of high-level hard drinking are only one way by which we can sense the vivid color of those times.

Another way lies among the newspapers. Many of them were mean, witty, acid, literate, committed, frequently unfair and usually on the attack. When they disliked something —and many heartily disliked Confederation —they expressed their distaste with a combination of arrogance, style and bluntness. For instance, the St. Catharines *Evening Journal* disputed the idea that the voice of the people is the voice of God in the following terms:

'We don't desire our institutions to be the playthings of an irresponsible Executive, or the footballs of a senseless and levelling rabble, or the targets for wide-mouthed fanatics to shoot their mad ravings at . . .'

And the *Barrie Examiner,* discussing U.S. legislatures, said they were all filled with 'demagogues, prizefighters and other specimens of the genus vagabond, who can handle a bowie knife much better than a pen'. The Halifax *Morning Chronicle* described French-Canadians as 'the half-civilized people of the sterile shores of the Saguenay, the shivering squatters way up by the Temiscouata Lake', and the *Stratford Beacon* gave its readers this unsparing definition of the last hours of the

George Brown campaigning for election

Confederation debate of 1865:

'. . . the House was in an unmistakably seedy condition, having, as it was positively declared, eaten the saloon keeper clean out, drunk him entirely dry, and got all the fitful naps of sleep that the benches along the passages could be made to yield . . . Men with the strongest constitutions for Parliamentary twaddle were sick of the debate, and the great bulk of the members were scattered about the building, with an up-all-night, get-tight-in-morning air, impatient for the sound of the division bell. It rang at last, at quarter past four, and the jaded representatives of the people swarmed in to the discharge of the most important duty of all their lives.'

The Saint John *Weekly Telegraph* was even tougher on the New Brunswick Assembly:

'There they sit day after day, quietly pocketing the $4 and other perquisites, eating and sleeping and drinking at the public expense, but never, except probably once in the term, are they found opening their lips in the interests of the people whom they represent . . . We have seen a member of the Legislature before now, not only ignorant, possessing information of no higher grade than that afforded by an Engine House education, but filthy in personal appearance, squirting tobacco juice on every side of him . . .'

The newspapers were rough enough, but the things they said were probably mild compared to the language that must have flown when political enemies met face-to-face. In 1866, J.-B.-E. Dorion, *l'enfant terrible* of the Canadian Assembly, complained that an Ottawa editor had slapped him across the face; and William Miller, MLA, publicly pummelled the editor of the Halifax *Sun* outside the Nova Scotia Assembly. Only a year before that a fearful row had blown up in the Canadian House because one of two MLAs, who happened to meet behind the Speaker's throne, decided it was time to settle a long-standing grudge between them. He grabbed the other man's nose and gave it a powerful yank.

Moreover, though these incidents involved public figures, they were small stuff beside the awful mayhem that frequently sprang

Doorway of John A. Macdonald's Kingston law office

Desk and chair used by Macdonald

George Brown and John A. Macdonald discuss Confederation

out of public meetings and election-day brawls. In the Newfoundland election of 1861 people suffered violent deaths in Harbour Grace and Harbour Main, and it wasn't until a hundred troops came over from Halifax that things finally settled down.

In short, those distinguished and stuffy-looking gents whom we credit with inventing Canada were playing their politics in a rough, tough, fast league (and it is hardly surprising that, now and then, they liked to unwind at raucous parties). But even though public affairs were frequently corrupt, and even though the prejudices men held were deep and bitter, the motives of the politicians were not all negative, and their emotions were not all ignoble. When George Brown, the enormously respected editor of the Toronto *Globe*, agreed to enter a coalition government with John A. Macdonald, he made one of the most dramatic speeches in Canadian history. After he'd finished, members from both sides of the House swarmed around him. Some of the French members, it is said, reached up to kiss him on both cheeks.

That was on June 22, 1864, and because the events of that day were emotional, happy, surprising and mysteriously ennobling, it was as good a time as any to begin the story of that whole emotional, happy, surprising and mysteriously ennobling summer and fall of 1864.

Again and again in the years before July 1, 1867, the cause of Confederation would drop right out of sight but, later, the extraordinary fact that it had actually happened would seem to spring directly from the talks, the new friendships and the jolly travelling times of the season of 1864. It was then—among the champagne glasses as well as the minutes of the meetings—that the Confederation fever struck a few important men, and they could never shake it.

The campaign for Confederation was an exercise in the hard sell at the backwoods level. The salesmen were the politicians of the new coalition government that now ran the union of Canada West (Ontario) and Canada East (Quebec); they dearly hoped that some form of federation with all the colonies of British North America would bail them out of their own hopeless political stalemate. The customers—and they were a mightily suspicious bunch—were supposed to be Nova Scotia, New Brunswick and Prince Edward Island.

The salesmen knew very little about their potential customers. Only two or three Cana-

WOMEN'S DRESS 1866~1880

1877

dian politicians had even the slightest first-hand knowledge of the Maritimes. D'Arcy McGee reported that a Canadian who was curious about Maritimers earnestly asked him, 'What kind of people are they?' as though Maritimers were Mongolian tribesmen or Hottentot warriors.

Maritimers were almost as ignorant of Canada, and what little they did know about it they didn't like much. Canada was a land of rebellions, a place where people had hurled rotten eggs at a governor-general, the jaded home of railway scandals, broken faith and messy government. John A. and his sales team had a monumental selling job ahead of them.

They began on June 30, 1864, by asking permission to attend a conference on Maritime Union. Now, the Maritimes had been mumbling aimlessly about a union among themselves for several years and they'd recently given an unenthusiastic airing to the idea of holding a conference on the matter. They had not decided where to hold it, or when, or who should attend and yet, here were the Canadians asking themselves in already. The Maritimes obliged and announced they'd have their conference September 1 in Charlottetown, and the Canadians could come along.

Meanwhile, and quite by chance, a hundred-odd jolly good fellows from Canada were preparing to make a big, fast, back-slapping, hand-shaking tour through New Brunswick and Nova Scotia. Businessmen in Halifax and Saint John had invited them on this mission of discovery and, early in August, they set out—D'Arcy McGee, 23 newspapermen, 18 members of the Canadian Legislative Council, 32 members of the Assembly, and roughly 40 other men of some distinction.

Saint John was an ambitious, lively, relaxed, money-conscious, cigar-smoking, theatre-going town. It had a pleasantly American atmosphere and it was the biggest city in the Maritimes. The Canadians, as they sailed up from Maine on an evening in early August, were astonished to find thousands upon thousands of cheering people gathered at the docks to welcome them. There was a levee at the Court House the next morning, and that night the Saint John Chamber of Commerce laid on a button-popping banquet.

A couple of days later the Canadians boarded a special steamer, the *Anna Augusta* and—with the band of the 15th Regiment pumping away and the French Canadians singing old canoeing songs and swinging imaginary paddles—they sailed up through a fragrant summer day, up through one of the most beautiful river valleys in North America, to Fredericton. 'The heat was gently softened by the summer breeze,' the Saint John *Morning Telegraph* reported, 'and the fleecy clouds which hung in the sky above us seemed but the shadows of the glorious earth.'

The same magical weather and sweet good

spirit clung to the Canadians throughout their entire three-week trip. In Halifax they attended a 'bonnet hop' aboard Admiral Sir James Hope's 81-gun flagship, *HMS Duncan*. They gleefully accepted invitations to the Royal Halifax Yacht Club's annual 'Hodge-Podge and Chowder Party'. This function began mid-morning on yet another golden day. Bunting streamed from the yachts and a good wind drove them up Bedford Basin. The whole mob of Canadians and their east-coast hosts disembarked, walked up to the pretty grounds of the Duke of Kent's old estate, and started to dig into the great feast that was laid out there on the grass. Soon they were feeling very good. The Toronto *Leader* reported:

'. . . leap-frog at once became the order of the day and a lively scene ensued. Members of the Upper House backed members of the Lower House with an agility that was wonderful. Blue-noses sprang over Canadians with a shriek of delight. Canadians bounded over New Brunswickers and tripped over Nova Scotians. Editors and correspondents mingled in the fray and perilled their valuable persons by seeking the bubble reputation . . .'

McGee made a speech, Joseph Howe made a speech, the pipers showed up, the Scotsmen danced the Highland fling, and it wasn't until a full moon was climbing over Bedford Basin that the party sailed back downtown.

Two nights later there was another one of those fierce exercises in happy gluttony

71

which the Victorian gentlemen of British North America regarded as ceremonial dinners and, shortly after that, *HMS Lily*, a 700-ton corvette, took the Canadians for a short cruise beyond the harbor. Returning, the Toronto *Leader* reported, 'Nature smiled upon us . . . on one side the city of Halifax looking resplendent in the fullness of the noon-day sun, and on the Dartmouth side . . . the fields still green and lively with pretty cottages peeping out from charming clusters of trees.'

In the third week of August, the Canadians went back home. They'd been stunned by the weather, the beauty, the hospitality and the goodwill of the Maritimers and, for the east coast's part, the Saint John *Morning Telegraph* was speaking for a good many influential and persuasive men when it said, 'the Canadians are good fellows and a jolly set, and . . . we are sorry to part with them . . .'

This sunny excursion did not, of course, convince the Maritimes that they should join Canada in Confederation. Nor did it come anywhere near blowing away forever their distrust of the Canadian character, or their wariness concerning the larger political motives of Canadians. But it did convince some Maritimers that Canadians, as a whole, were not such bad chaps, not quite so foreign as they'd supposed. Canadians, too, liked good times, good food, good liquor, leap-frog and laughs. The trip ended only a few days before the Charlottetown Conference began and, though its timing was pure coincidence, it turned out to be something of an ice-breaker for the meeting, an atmosphere-warmer, a squirt of sweet oil to lubricate intercolonial frictions.

The *Queen Victoria*, carrying eight Canadian cabinet ministers, left Quebec on the evening of Monday, August 29 and, after a mild and sunny passage down the St. Lawrence and along the New Brunswick coast, steamed into Charlottetown on Thursday afternoon, September 1. The Canadians, by then, had apparently worked out their Confederation scheme and their Confederation pitch in some detail. All eight of them were highly familiar with the plan, had a clear idea of what each one should say, and a powerful recognition of their common purpose. One of them, the Grit newspaper editor George Brown offered a vivid description of the earliest stages in the Canadian 'invasion':

'Having dressed ourselves in correct style, our two boats were lowered man-of-war fashion, and being each duly manned with four oarsmen and a boatswain, dressed in blue uniforms, hats, belts, etc. in regular style, we pulled away from shore and landed like Mr. Christopher Columbus who had the precedence of us in taking possession of portions of the American continent.'

The Charlottetown Conference met that afternoon, promptly deferred the whole phony question of Maritime Union, and agreed to hear the Canadians for four days. A week later, the Saint John *Morning Telegraph* reported that the arguments of John A. Macdonald, George Brown, George-Etienne Cartier and the other Canadians were 'almost irresistible' and that 'our own delegates are still more favorable to (BNA) Union than they were, and as they consult and converse with the Canadians the difficulties in the matter of detail vanish.'

One of the things that undoubtedly helped obscure the detail was the convivial or, to hear the subsequent critics of Confederation tell it, the downright indulgent quality of the extracurricular activities at Charlottetown. On Friday, the day after the Canadians arrived, Provincial Secretary W. H. Pope held a luscious buffet lunch at his house and, on Saturday afternoon, the Canadians countered with what was perhaps the most significant piece of shipboard hospitality in the history of Canada. The formal work was over till Monday morning. At four in the afternoon aboard the *Queen Victoria* the champagne began to pop. Cartier spoke, Brown spoke, McGee spoke with brilliant wit, the corks kept on flying, men gathered warm confidence and the hard-nosed Maritimers

A mid-Victorian family stroll

actually began to believe that, yes, some day, a Confederation of the colonies of British North America might actually come to pass.

It was at this sunny, extravagant, mid-afternoon bash on the decks of a little steamer in Charlottetown's harbor that Confederation began to win converts, and to inspire them with a sense of mission.

The Canadians finished their formal presentation on Tuesday, the Maritime delegates abandoned all consideration of Maritime Union, and the conference adjourned to Halifax. But first the Canadians entertained the lieutenant-governor of Prince Edward Island and flocks of local ladies; the conference spent a day at the warm, beautiful beaches on the north shore; and that night everyone stayed up all night at the great ball whose orgiastic activities so deeply offended *Ross's Weekly*.

The conference stayed in Halifax only long enough to adjourn to Saint John, to agree to a further conference at Quebec in October, and to attend a public dinner where once again the huge amounts of food seemed to reflect everyone's idea of the occasion's huge amount of importance. Then they rolled on to Saint John where, at still another banquet, the New Brunswickers toasted the others, everyone bellowed out 'For they are jolly good fellows,' and Cartier staggered through 'God Save the Queen' in both French and English. The next morning they moved on to Fredericton and from there they all went home to get ready for the Quebec Conference.

The Charlottetown Conference, for all the sniping it was already undergoing at the hands of the anti-Confederation press, had witnessed the first appearance in British North America of an undeniably authentic national spirit.

At first the atmosphere at Quebec was considerably more depressing. It rained there day after day and, though the Charlottetown talks had enabled the delegates to reach large agreement on the virtues and general principles of Confederation, the Quebec Conference could not easily agree on the details. By the fourth day the Toronto *Globe* was reporting that 'everyone here has had a fit of the blues.'

Then once more the Canadian government came to the rescue, this time with another ball. There were 800 guests. They danced quadrilles, polkas and waltzes and the Canadian cabinet hurled themselves into the spirit of the function with a gusto that inspired a Maritime delegate to describe them as 'the most inveterate dancers I have ever seen. They do not seem to miss a dance during the live long night.'

He went on. 'They are cunning fellows; and there's no doubt that it is all done for a political purpose; they know that if they can dance themselves into the affections of the wives and daughters of the country, the men will certainly become an easy conquest.'

And there was no shortage of wives and daughters. There were plenty of beautiful French-Canadian women but, more surprising, the Maritime delegates apparently regarded the conference as a choice opportunity to show their daughters to colonial society. Charles Tupper, the premier of Nova Scotia, brought his wife and daughter. So did the Nova Scotia Liberal A. G. Archibald, and George Cole of Prince Edward Island. R. J. Dickey of Nova Scotia, Charles Fisher, W. H. Steeves and J. H. Gray of New Brunswick all brought their daughters.

It was not altogether surprising then that, one week after the government ball, the bachelors of Quebec threw a Bachelors' Ball. Nor that George Sala, a famous correspondent for the London *Daily Telegraph*, included the ladies in his description of the east-coast representation: 'Nova Scotians, Newfoundlanders, New Brunswickers and Prince Edward Islanders, stalwart Saxon-looking yeomen, with comely wives and pretty daughters . . .'

There were other good times in Quebec. The Board of Trade held a memorable Quebec-style feast at Russell's Hotel. After the conference ended, the various hotel claims

Fashions of 1860, right, dispense with the frivolity of 1816 dress

against the Canadian government totalled $15,000. 'The Canadians—who must, after all, be generous hearted fellows—appear to have great faith in the power of good feed, champagne and torch light, as much more potent than dry argument,' said the Fredericton *Head Quarters*. 'They seem to think that turning the head is a synonymous phrase with convincing the mind.'

The delegates all stayed in the St. Louis Hotel and, according to Joseph McCully of Nova Scotia, they were 'a very merry party'. The *Quebec Daily News* chided Liberal George Brown for becoming 'as lithe and gay as the merriest courtier of the old Tory compact',

and A. J. Smith, leader of the Confederation-haters in New Brunswick, could invariably draw a laugh at public meetings with remarks like this: 'They had nice times going up (to Quebec) and nicer after they got there . . . dinners, balls, champagne, suppers, and only when surrounded with such influences were they fit to form a new empire.'

Near the end of the month the conference moved west. No fewer than a thousand guests attended a conference ball in Montreal. The delegates met for another highly amiable lunch the next day and then—on a soft, golden, late-autumn day—a steamer took them north to Ottawa. There, dense crowds filled the streets, a torchlight parade guided the delegates to their hotel and, as one of the Nova Scotians said over lunch at the half-finished Parliament Buildings the next day, 'We were indeed received like conquerors, like warriors returned from a great victory.'

The train trip to Toronto was even more astonishing. All along the route crowds turned out to cheer and wave handkerchiefs and, at one stop late in the afternoon, the delegates downed bumpers of champagne on the station platform. At Toronto four brass bands, blazing torches, exotic firecrackers and

thousands of people accompanied them to the Queen's Hotel. Some of the Fathers spoke from the hotel balcony to the crowds below, and the excitement in the streets did not die down till almost midnight. 'We have been received with continued ovation,' said McCully of Nova Scotia. 'It has been one Carnival, from the beginning until now.'

It was, of course, more than a carnival and when the long and frequently tense daytime discussions of the Quebec Conference were all over, George Brown expressed his joy at its more sober accomplishments. He wrote to his wife: 'All right!!! Conference through at six o'clock this evening—constitution adopted—a most creditable document—a

Dress fashions in 1866

1866

complete reform of all the abuses and injustices we have complained of.'

Brown had a right to be proud of the constitution but there was another achievement of '64, and it occurred on a more personal level.

It was the growth of an atmosphere among a few men, a shared experience, a contagious dream, an idea that took hold of different men at different times . . . at the 5th glass of champagne . . . the 16th oyster . . . the 350th blazing torch . . . the 4,000th mile . . . the 10,000th cheering voice.

Somewhere during that summer, this handful of politicians, many of whom had been strangers to one another, all found themselves hoping and thinking and working together for something that held more grandeur than any ambition they'd ever known before. Confederation, and many of their own political careers, still faced far more painful setbacks than any of them could foretell at the end of 1864 but, all the same, the months from June to November were a sweet time to remember.

For most of the Fathers, however, the months that followed '64 were something else. In New Brunswick the defeat in 1865 of Confederationist Leonard Tilley's government seemed, for a while, to have sunk the cause forever, both there and throughout the Maritimes. The cause of Confederation brought about the political ruin of some of its most distinguished advocates in Prince Edward Island and, though the island did finally join Confederation in 1873 it would take the tough, resilient and stubborn Newfoundlanders until the middle of the following century to reconcile themselves to joining Canada.

But ingenuity, luck, courage and the gathering weight of opinion in London began to work on behalf of the Fathers' vision. In December, 1866, delegates from Nova Scotia and New Brunswick joined the Canadians in a final conference at the Westminster Palace Hotel, London. The Quebec meeting had achieved a general agreement on the legal and financial basis for Confederation but some horse trading was still necessary. Moreover, Britain had some ideas of her own concerning the legislation that would establish what they all finally agreed to call 'the Dominion of Canada'.

The British North America Act was introduced to the British Parliament in March, 1867, and it passed with barely a ripple of debate. An anti-Confederation group from Nova Scotia, who'd camped in London during the winter and fought the scheme to the last hopeless minute, bitterly contrasted the uneventful passage of the BNA Act to the eagerness with which the British MPs plunged into a debate on a new dog tax. On July 1, 1867, a royal proclamation brought the Act into force for the four founding provinces of Nova Scotia, New Brunswick, Ontario and Quebec.

All over the new country, July 1 dawned clear and quite warm. 'With the first dawn of this gladsome summer morn,' began the Toronto *Globe*, 'we hail this birthday of a new nationality. A united British America takes its place among the nations of the world.' Newspapers from Halifax to Sarnia talked about 'our new destiny,' and even Summerside, Prince Edward Island, wished Canada well. And—though black crepe hung in the streets of Yarmouth and Halifax, though the Halifax *Morning Chronicle* published a bitter epitaph and though all but one of Nova Scotia's 19 members of the House of Commons were anti-Confederationists—ceremonial guns were booming in Quebec, Toronto, Ottawa, Fredericton and, yes, Halifax too. There were parades, and the sound of brass everywhere. There was a swelling nationalism in the eastern speeches, and stories that the West Coast favored joining Confederation. Flags were out. The sun was shining. The day was as beautiful as any summer day has ever been and, in the several cities of the Dominion of Canada, the friends of Confederation began to mark the great occasion by cracking oysters and lifting champagne to their lips.

Captain John Palliser, left, and Sir James Hector exploring the west

Consolidation

One country sea to sea

by ROBERT COLLINS

MONDAY last, 1st July, was the birthday of the Canadian Dominion. It was proclaimed as a public holiday and to some extent was observed in this town as such, but by no means as a day of rejoicing. Throughout the day, numerous flags were displayed half-mast, some of them draped in mourning . . . In several localities the men wore black weeds on their hats . . . An effigy of Dr. Tupper was suspended by the neck all afternoon on the spot known as The Devil's Half Acre and in the evening was burnt side by side with a live rat. Another effigy of Dr. Tupper was burnt on the Parade . . .'

(Yarmouth, N.S., *Herald*, July 4, 1867)

And so Canada limped into Confederation. Bells pealed, fireworks popped, troops paraded, speeches rolled on and on in Ontario, Quebec and New Brunswick. But Nova Scotians—those most prosperous of Canadians with their shipping, fishing and trade with the Yankees—came in kicking and screaming. They were sure their premier, Charles Tupper, had sold out to central Canada. For yielding a measure of revenue and independence to Ottawa they'd get a federal grant of 40 cents per head—about the price of a sheepskin, roared their fiery spokesman, Joseph Howe. Nova Scotia wanted out.

It was only one of the splitting headaches facing the fathers of our country that day. Confederation was not an end but a beginning. Ahead lay four critical years. Not until 1871 would Nova Scotia be placated; the pushy Americans finally discouraged from trying to take over Canada; those crazy Irish raiders, the Fenians, turned away for the last time; and restless Manitoba, far-off British Columbia and the sprawling Territories pulled together to more or less assure the nation's survival.

They were troubled, violent years, but they were also glorious, rollicking years. They were times when nobody doubted the future of the Empire, much less the survival of mankind; when all stout fellows rose on cue to offer 'Three cheers!' for the Queen, the commanding general, the newest MP or almost anybody; when gentlemen wrote love letters to ladies that said, 'Tomorrow I shall hasten to the presence of her from whom I hope I may never henceforth be parted . . .'

If they now seem like incredibly naive times, it is because most Canadians then were simple outdoorsmen, thinly spread across the wilderness, in a relatively uncomplicated age. There were only 3,300,000 souls in the four provinces, 75 per cent of them in Ontario and Quebec, and most were very close to nature. The Maritimes, to be sure, had bankers, lawyers, flocks of little universities and newspapers, and a lively literature led by Thomas Haliburton's waggish clockmaker, Sam Slick. But their strength was in ships and the sea. It was the last day of the wooden

Red River cart

ship and Nova Scotia built hundreds of them. The Halifax fish market featured 16 different species. Nets lay like cobwebs on the grass in every village. Lobster flopped in the shallows of the Miramichi River with every outgoing tide; you could buy 100 for 50 cents.

It was the same in the central provinces. Montreal, true enough, was a sophisticated city of 100,000 where merchant princes lived amidst cushiony carpets, velvet draperies and crystal chandeliers. Quebec City's 60,000 included students and priests, soldiers and gen-

try. But the backbone of Quebec province was the habitant, a cheerful God-fearing soul in cap, vest, breeches and *bottes indiennes;* long, low whitewashed stone houses; villages with saintly names that rang like church bells; tiny slots of farms hugging that great highway, the St. Lawrence River.

Ontario had Toronto, 50,000 and growing fast, full of Tories, churches, bars, Orangemen, Methodists and merchants. Its census included clerks, carpenters, saddlers, brewers, shoemakers, blacksmiths, booksellers, bankers, grocers, hotelkeepers. Both it and Montreal had gas lights, boardwalks, cobbled streets and horse-drawn streetcars. Stage coaches were being relegated to back roads. For $10 first class, $8 second class, you could ride the Grand Trunk Railway between Montreal and Toronto any day but Sunday—a jolting, grimy, cinder-splattered ordeal with the funnel-shaped smokestack billowing sooty clouds. Still, you made it in 14 hours, a near-miracle in those days. Surely *this* was civilization.

But these were exceptions. In all four provinces, countrymen in their baggy homespun outnumbered the frock-coated citymen, eight to one. The rich odor of fresh-turned sod, the tang of new-cut wood was everywhere. Beyond, in the Canada-yet-to-be, the Red River settlement at Fort Garry was a wild collection of Indians, grass, half-breeds, buffalo, unkempt farmers in buckskins and sheer hard-

ship. Grasshoppers stripped the crops that first summer of Confederation; by winter, the settlers were eating horses, even cats. Here the only 'trains' were Red River carts, bound together with tough dried buffalo hide, ox-drawn, devoid of nails or grease, screeching south or west. When the ruts grew too deep they shifted one cart wheel onto fresh sod and so, in time, parallel tracks moved off to infinity, through Indian and missionary country, finally to a fort perched high over the North Saskatchewan.

'The establishment at Edmonton boasts of a windmill, a blacksmith's forge and carpenter's shop. The boats required for the annual voyage to York Factory in Hudson Bay are built and mended here. . . Wheat grows luxuriantly. . . There are about 30 families living in the Fort . . .'

(Journal of English travellers W. B. Cheadle and Viscount Milton, 1865)

Horse racing at Fort Garry, Manitoba

LOWER FORT GARRY

Hudson's Bay Company store and fur loft, built in 1833

Dog teams in front of Hudson's Bay Company agent's house

Beyond lay the Rockies; then the Cariboo gold fields now dwindling to nothing; then the newly united colonies of Vancouver Island and British Columbia, heavily in debt yet hungrily eyed by the United States.

The west was not yet Canadian, but it was not American, either. The 49th parallel had been recognized as the border between the United States and British colonies in the west ever since the Treaty of Paris in 1783, although at that time it had been meant to reach only to the Mississippi River. When it was discovered that the Mississippi rose farther south, the two governments took the sensible course of extending the boundary west to the Rockies in 1818. The Americans wanted to push it straight through to the Pacific, but the British were not yet ready to surrender Oregon, although they agreed to do just that in 1846.

The idea of stitching all this wilderness into the new country was beyond the ken of most Canadians. A Halifax clergyman, soliciting funds for the Red River famine victims, said Nova Scotians 'would have given quite as intelligently had the sufferers been in Central Abyssinia'. Canadians of 1867 had other worries, some of them remarkably like ours.

They feared the Americans, many of whom, having finished the Civil War, wanted to annex Canada. The pop song of the day was the Yankees' '*Tramp, Tramp, Tramp The Boys Are Marching*' and although Canadians sang it, the way they always sing American songs, it gave them a queasy feeling.

They also fretted over contemporary manners and morals. Teenagers were less obedient, more pampered and more interested in sex (referred to as 'the nameless sin') than in stricter pioneer days. Staunch church-goers all, Canadians viewed women's fashions with mingled delight and alarm. The voluminous skirt, nipped-in waist and billowing bodice displaying a wide acreage of bare bosom that was the fashion throughout the period was surely sinful and maybe even a health hazard. 'That our daughters here in frigid and

changeable climate should expose to the chilling winds a vital part of the body, is one of the evils of fashion which should be discountenanced by every mother, father and brother.'

(Anonymous writer, London, Ont., 1882)

Women bared their *décolletage* anyway, and, when the winds grew sharp, stuffed newspapers under their coatfronts. They could be forgiven this little show of femininity; women's life for the most part was drudgery, especially in the country. They made everything, from tallow soap to elderberry shoe polish. The family wash was a soak-on-Monday-scrub-on-Tuesday horror that the newfangled washing machine had not yet alleviated. Cooking was forsaking the fireplace for a cast iron stove but it was still primitive; to tell if the oven was hot enough for a cake, the housewife was advised to 'hold your arm in and count to 40'. (If she could only count to 20 before pulling out, the oven was hot enough for pumpkin pie.) She was also urged to burn dishcloths when they became 'black and stiff and smell like a barnyard'. Bedbugs were everywhere. Open sewers and outdoor privies were common even in the cities. Bathtubs were for the rich. Most people washed their hands, face and feet in that order of priority and countered other

Protestant Church & Mission School, Red River 1820

body odors with scented pomades and lotions. Anyway, a man with an honest smell was likely an honest man. Daughters were warned that the city dandy who carried scented sachets in his pockets was doubtless disguising some evil: booze, tobacco or bad breath.

If Canadians of that era were less fastidious than us they were a sight more neighborly. In Quebec they carried neighborliness to the extreme, with the *charivari*. On a wedding night the yokels blackened their faces, donned grotesque costumes and set up an awful din of horns, drums and banging pots and pans outside the newlyweds' home. If the groom refused to invite them in for a drink he might be forcibly removed, tarred, feathered and ridden on a rail.

In Ontario, the ubiquitous 'bee' was one way of mixing business with pleasure. The gentler kind—corn husking, apple paring, quilting—were good excuses for 'sparking'. If a boy happened to find a colored kernel in a corn cob it entitled him to kiss his girl. If she tossed a curling apple peel that spelled his initial—good omen! And a quilting bee might end with young men dropping in for tea and being roguishly tossed in the newly finished quilt.

Barn raisings were lustier affairs, featuring heavy work, drinking, fighting, the occasional killing, and eating.

'Our men worked well until dinner time when after washing in the lake they all sat down to the rude board which I had prepared for them loaded with the best fare that could be produced in the bush. Pea soup, legs of pork, venison, eel, and raspberry pie, plenty of potatoes and whisky to wash them down, besides a large iron kettle of tea . . .'

(Susanna Moodie: *Roughing it in the Bush*, 1871)

After the food, wives and girl friends would join in and dance until dawn. Or maybe the men drifted off to the general store to sit around whittling, spitting (tobacco or spruce gum) and talking politics. Politics were a live issue that first autumn of Confederation. In the August election Sir John A. Macdonald carried three of the provinces and formed a coalition cabinet. But it was an uneasy victory. In Nova Scotia, only Tupper of all the Confederationists was elected.

It was merely part of the crushing load that John A. carried with grace. For all his whisky-drinking human frailty, the homely 52-year-old statesman was surely the only man with the wisdom, wit, diplomacy and sheer staying power to hold Canada together in those times.

'He can throw off a weight of business in a wonderfully short time. Oftentimes he comes in with a very moody brow, tired and oppressed, his voice weak, his step slow; and 10 minutes after he is making clever jokes and laughing like any schoolboy, with his hands in his pockets and his head thrown back.'

(Diary of Lady Susan Agnes Macdonald, July, 1867)

The MPs gathered in November for the first Parliament. Ottawa was a scruffy town of 21,000, short on accommodation and social graces, noted mainly for riotous brawls whenever the river log-drivers hit town. The new Parliament Buildings were by far the most imposing sight, even though the clock tower reminded John A. of 'a cowbell'. But then cowbell architecture was the vogue in every courthouse or city hall in the land.

For a while the Nova Scotians, led by the brilliant Howe—a rumpled man with coarse features, untidy grey hair and a tongue that could bring a cheering crowd to its feet—didn't unduly harass the government. Christmas came, a bountiful time in this productive land. City markets were glutted with frozen carcasses of pigs, sheep, deer, ducks, geese, chickens, turkey. The fun was plain and ample too. Sleigh rides, hay rides, ice boating and skating.

Nowhere were winter sports more popular than in Quebec province. The Saturday downtown parade of sleighs pulled by high stepping horses was a Montreal 'special'. In the Victoria indoor rink, hundreds skated

During Red River flood Rev. John Black preaches at Stony Mountain, Manitoba

on the 200-by-80-foot ice surface. Peel Street was turned over to tobogganing every evening.

At night, by the light of candles or lanterns of the new petroleum lamps, taffy pulls, spelling bees, whist, euchre, cribbage, home theatricals, musicales, recitations. And, of course, the question of decorating Christmas trees.

'Do not load its green boughs with sugar candies . . . You can make your Christmas tree with the healthful gifts of Nature . . . Apples, pears, grapes, nuts and other fruits that the little ones love. You can add lumps of real sugar, white and clear as crystal, if sweets are indispensable; and there are sugar candies honestly prepared from good sugar

85

C.W. JEFFERYS

and made beautiful without coloring.'

(Sarah Hale: *Manners*, 1868)

New Year's was a riproaring time of parties, house visits and, in Quebec, the traditional blessing of the entire family by the head of the household. For John A. and his government, though, the New Year turned bitter. Nova Scotia seemed determined to abandon Canada. Joseph Howe sailed to England to seek the mother country's support. Macdonald sent Tupper after him to counter his arguments and try to reason with him. The debate raged on in the House. Macdonald was fortunate to have a supporter like D'Arcy McGee, a darkly handsome Irish poet, journalist and Parliamentarian, one of the greatest orators in Canadian history. McGee had become increasingly critical of the Fenians, those American Irish who in their bumbling attempts to free Ireland from Britain had already made several abortive attacks on Canada. And in McGee, too, the 'Canada First' movement, a little show of nationalism in the late Sixties, found its inspiration.

C.W. JEFFERYS

TOLL GATE

But now, on the night of April 6, 1868, McGee was concluding a stirring speech on the Nova Scotia problem: 'I have great reliance on the mellowing effects of time. Time will heal all existing irritations; time will mellow and refine all points of contrast that seem so harsh today . . .' He sat down to warm applause.

'Ottawa: The Hon. T. D. McGee was assassinated at half past two this morning. He stayed in the House till 2 o'clock, made a long and eloquent speech, walked home to

summer John A. followed up with shrewd strategy: he visited Halifax with George-Etienne Cartier, Tupper, and Ontario Premier John Sandfield Macdonald, an intimate friend of Howe and one-time anti-Confederationist. They reasoned and cajoled. Howe, too loyal a Canadian to permit Nova Scotia's annexation by the U.S. (a distinct possibility), gave in. Ultimately he accepted a cabinet post in the Macdonald government and helped Tupper sweep the province in the next federal election.

The Toronto, first locomotive built in Ontario

his boarding house. Arrived there he put his hand to open the door with his latchkey when someone behind him fired at him. The shot passed through the back of his neck and came out at his mouth . . . He was dead when found.'

(Toronto *Globe,* April 7, 1868)

John A. rushed to the scene and helped carry the body indoors. A Fenian was later arrested and convicted of the murder, but historians suspect others were involved. It was a blow for the government; McGee at 43 had been in the prime of political life.

But the Confederation forces were winning Nova Scotia anyway. In London, Howe had received scant support from the British. That

Canada's government was far too preoccupied that summer of 1868 to notice a curious juxtaposition of events in the Red River settlement. In July, Louis Riel, a young Métis with thick curly black hair and brooding intelligent eyes, returned to his native St. Boniface after studying for the priesthood in Montreal. The Métis were a people apart—half white, half Indian. Neither nomadic nor settled, they developed a way of life that was entirely their own, and they nursed a fierce pride in their hybrid race. Riel, a fiery speaker and ardent student of politics, was destined never to be a priest. He took a traditional Métis job driving a Red River cart train and began to rediscover the problems of his people. Their old way of life—trapping,

Métis hunting buffalo on the prairies

working the cart trains, raising cattle on small rectangular farms running French-style to the banks of the Red River—was about to vanish under an onslaught of settlement. Already a federal government crew was starting a road between Fort Garry and Fort William, the first hint that Canada would soon buy Rupert's Land, including what is now Manitoba, from the Hudson's Bay Company.

One of the road builders was Thomas Scott, an Irish-Canadian Orangeman with a quick temper and considerable disdain for Indians and Métis. Scott and others fell in with a third player in the Red River drama: Dr. John Christian Schultz, an Ontario hustler who'd staked out great tracts of land, aspired to government and wanted to see the west opened to settlers.

If this simmering stew was little known to John A. and his followers, it was a total blank to the average Canadian. Summer life in Canada was hard work on weekdays but never on Sunday. That was the day every living soul went on picnics. Picnics? Gastronomical orgies!

'One joint cold roast beef, 1 joint cold boiled beef, 2 ribs of lamb, 2 shoulders of lamb, 4 roast fowls, 2 roast ducks, 1 ham, 2 veal and ham pies, 2 pigeon pies, 6 medium lobster, 18 lettuces, 6 baskets of salad, 3-4 doz. plain pastry biscuits, 2 doz. fruit turnovers, 4 doz. cheesecakes, 3 doz. plain biscuits, 6 lbs. butter, 3 doz. quarts of ale, 2 doz. each ginger beer, soda water, lemonade, 6 sherry. . . .'

(Partial picnic recipe for 40 persons, 1860s)

Sumptuous though they were, those feasts of a century ago would probably not appeal to our tastes today. The bread was gritty because milling was imperfect. Eggs frequently had a gamey taste, since hens ate anything they could catch. Milk might be tainted with turnip or wild herbs. Sugar had a molasses flavor. Butter quickly went rancid. Anyway, if you believed one London, Ont., doctor, who later gained fame for his yearly almanac, medicines and advice on just about every-

thing, people of 1868 just over-stuffed themselves.

'In the good old days of corn bread and crust coffee, there was but little trouble with Dyspepsia but since the days of fashionable intemperance, both in eating and drinking, such as spirituous liquors, wines, beers, also tea and coffee, hot bread or biscuit, high seasoned food, overloading the stomach at meals, and constant eating and drinking between meals, excessive venery, want of outdoor exercise, all have a tendency to debilitate the stomach and bring on or cause Dyspepsia. . .'

(Dr. Chase's Recipes, London, Ont., 1868)

Politically, the Yankees were giving John A. a different kind of heartburn. Since the Civil War they had pestered England for payment of damages caused to Northern shipping by the Confederate privateer, *Alabama*, built in English shipyards and sold by England to the South. Several highly-placed Americans suggested Canada would be an acceptable payment. If not *all* of it at least the entire northwest, or B.C., or both, thereby giving the U.S. a handy corridor to its new possession, Alaska.

This latest piece of Yankee audacity infuriated most Canadians. By early 1869 'Johnny Canuck' became part of the Canadian image. He showed up in the Montreal humor magazine, *Grinchuckle*, as a clean-cut square-jawed type in unidentifiable uniform, vaguely resembling Hollywood's idea of a Royal Canadian Mountie. In his first cartoon appearance Johnny Canuck (then labelled 'Young Canada') kicked a rascally Uncle Sam out of Canada. The same sentiment ran high on the west coast.

Tune: Tramp! Tramp! Tramp!

Come boys, let's sing a song
For the day it won't be long
When united to our country we will be
Then the Maple Leaf entwined
And the Beaver too, combined
With Old England's flag shall float upon the sea.

Tramp! Tramp! Tramp! The new Dominion
Now is knocking at the door
So goodbye dear Uncle Sam
As we do not care a clam
For your greenbacks or your bunkum any more.

(Cariboo, B.C., *Sentinel*, June 19, 1869)

The Red River settlement had no particular love for Uncle Sam either, but neither did it like Canada's high-handed treatment. The federal government had now bought Rupert's Land and the Northwest Territories—an enormous area covering the northern parts of Ontario and Quebec, half of Baffin Island, all of the prairies to the B.C. border, and the present Northwest Territories—from the Hudson's Bay Company for $1,500,000 and certain grants of land. Fort Garry was neither consulted nor informed of negotiations. Now,

On the Cariboo Road to the British Columbia gold fields

A western settler plows his first furrow

well ahead of the December 1, 1868, takeover date, federal land surveyors were tramping through the Red River settlement.

It was too much for the Métis. They were loyal to Canada but they refused to meekly cede their land to greedy Ontario settlers, already moving in. They organized a council, with Louis Riel as secretary. In the meantime the first governor-designate, William McDougall, a cold, intractable easterner, made his way west via the easier U.S. route with a 60-wagon entourage. As he prepared to enter Canada at the international boundary (he, too, ahead of the official takeover time) the Métis peaceably but firmly turned him back. Then Riel and 100 armed men took Fort Garry without a shot, elected an assembly (English and Métis were equally represented) and drafted a Bill of Rights asking for responsible provincial government, ownership of their own land and fair representation in Parliament. Riel strictly disciplined

his troops, even to making them take an oath of temperance. It was no rebellion of savages.

The December deadline passed. McDougall scurried over the border long enough to read a phony proclamation saying he'd taken over in the name of the Queen, scrambled back to safety and was subsequently fired. Riel's flag flew over Fort Garry. Back east the baffled federal government sent Donald Smith, a respected Hudson's Bay Company governor, to make peace with the Red River settlers.

The easterners meanwhile settled into another winter of plenty and pleasure. Theirs was no longer really a pioneer society. There were flour, woollen and saw mills; banks, insurance companies and a new postal system (letter rate three cents per half-ounce). Western Ontario had oil wells and salt works. Montreal had sugar refineries. And there were distilleries, brickyards, brewers, tanners, clothiers, cobblers, saddlers and, of course, merchants.

Pioneer prairie houses. A framed log house, left, and an Austrian immigrant's homestead

Timothy Eaton had opened his Toronto store the day before with a new approach in retailing: cash sales only and one clearly marked price. For a start he offered fancy dress goods at 10¢ per yard. Toronto girls

stocked up in a hurry. After all, one had to dress prettily for church; here's where one might meet a man; with luck he'd ask to see you home. Later, maybe, if your parents liked him, he'd take you sleigh riding or to a dance. Dances were all-night marathons, fortified with little snacks of chicken, turkey,

beef and oysters. There were polkas, jigs, hornpipes, Scottish and Irish reels, the quadrille, the Schottische and the waltz.

'If a lady waltzes with you, beware not to press her waist; you must only lightly touch it with the open palm of your hand lest you leave a disagreeable impression not only on her *ceinture* but on her mind.'

(*Rules of Etiquette*, Anonymous, 1857)

In the west, grimmer business was afoot. Riel had arrested some unruly Ontarians, including the notorious Schultz and the abrasive Scott, both of whom subsequently escaped to rouse more trouble. But Donald Smith arrived and one blustery January day in 1870 stood outdoors for five hours at 20 below zero, talking reason to a thousand colonists. They were impressed; they too wanted peace. They elected a new representative government, again with Riel as president. An English judge and French priest went east as delegates to work out orderly terms for the annexation of Rupert's Land. Success was near.

Then Thomas Scott joined an attempt to overthrow the Riel government and was arrested again. He incessantly berated his Métis guards, threatened Riel's life and incited other prisoners to do the same. Riel himself visited the cells to quiet him; Scott sprang on the Métis leader. Then Riel's self-control snapped. Impetuously, he held a trial, found Scott guilty of treason and sentenced him to death the next day. Smith and others begged him to reconsider. But at noon on March 4, Scott went before a firing squad.

'He said goodbye to the other prisoners, was led outside to the gate of the Fort with a white handkerchief covering his head. . . On descending the steps poor Scott said, 'This is cold blooded murder' . . . He continued in prayer . . . Then he knelt in the snow, said farewell, and immediately fell back pierced by three bullets which passed through his body . . . A man discharged his revolver at the sufferer, the ball, it is said, entering the eye and passing around the head . . .'

(Donald Smith's report on the execution)

News of the brutal act was three weeks reaching the east by letter and U.S. telegraph. English-Canadians were furious. With the Toronto *Globe*, they branded Riel a 'ruffian' and demanded an expedition to enforce peace in the west. Twelve thousand men were duly marshalled under Col. Garnet Wolseley for the long march.

Meanwhile the Province of Manitoba (Chippewa for 'The God that speaks') quiet-ly came into being on July 15, 1870. Riel waited, still hoping for a fair deal. He prepared a speech of welcome and trained the Fort's guards for a friendly salute. They had been assured by the Canadian government that Wolseley's troops came in peace.

But the grapevine reported otherwise. The troops were having a long hard trip by boat and portage. American and Canadian newspapers were ridiculing their slow progress and fanning their tempers. By the time they entered Manitoba they were mad at everything and everyone, especially the Métis. Riel, on the advice of his English friends, withdrew.

' . . . The whole country far and near was a sea of deep and clinging mud. There was nothing approaching a road in the whole territory so I had to forgo all pomp and circumstance of war and had once more to take to our boats and the dreary oar. We were all wet through, very cold and extremely cross and hungry . . . A cup of hot tea and a biscuit swallowed quickly and all were again at the oar by six a.m. August 24, 1870. The rain poured in buckets upon us and at places the country was under water. . .

'As I watched the muzzles of the fort guns I confess I hoped each moment to see a flash and hear a round shot rush by me . . . But

A prairie homesteader's dwelling of the 1880s

Riel had bolted and the fort gates were open. It was a sad disappointment to all ranks . . .'

(Report of Col. Wolseley)

So the 'rebellion' was put down. Wolseley's troops got drunk, looted, killed a few Métis and went home. Within weeks the settlement faced danger again, this time from the threat of yet another Fenian invasion. Riel (officially still in exile) urged his people to stand with the other Canadians against any attack, and himself quietly joined their ranks. But the Fenian army turned out to be 39 men who were hauled in by the U.S. army before they properly got over the border. Never again did the Fenians rise. Louis Riel did, though, in the 1880s, but for the time being he accepted a quiet gift of money from the federal government and faded into the U.S.

The west, now relatively peaceful, was still a bare-knuckled place. Manitoba's first elections were sprinkled with thugs, brawls and ugly accusations among candidates. Southwest, in what would some day be Alberta, two whisky traders built Fort Whoop-Up, on the Oldman River near modern Lethbridge, where Indians brought furs and went crazy on rotgut liquor. Places like Whoop-Up, with their accompanying abuses, eventually brought the Mounties to the west.

The entire plains region was ravaged by smallpox that fall and winter; an estimated 5,000 Cree and Blackfeet died.

'Our poor population is more than deci-

Father Lacombe persuades Chief Crowfoot to allow C.P.R. line through the Blackfeet reserve near Calgary

mated. As many as six burials a day at some of our stations. This dreadful epidemic had taken all compassion from the hearts of the Indians. The lepers of a new kind are removed at a distance from the others and sheltered with branches. There they witness the decomposition and putrefaction of their bodies several days before death . . .'

(Letter from Rev. Fr. Lacombe, Mission of St. Paul, to Bishop Tache, Winnipeg, 1870)

Of all the western regions, B.C. was perhaps the most tranquil. A Cariboo miner could go to night school for arithmetic, Spanish or English grammar. In Victoria you could buy a piano, life insurance or fishing tackle and they were at least bringing the fights indoors (with a 'sparring exhibition of muscular Christianity' Tuesday and Saturday nights in Armstrong's Old Lager Beer Cellar). The colony, having struck a deal with Canada which promised to give it a railway 10 years after entering Confederation, was eagerly awaiting official union in the summer of 1871. Rough or not, the country had survived the first critical years.

Or almost. There was still the constant harassment of the United States. The newest problem was fishing rights. American fishermen wanted free access to Canadian waters. Canada, with no reciprocal privileges, was quite properly charging a license fee. Americans had been ignoring it and Canadian and British ships had seized about 400 lawbreakers in three months. So, a British Commission, with John A. as the sole Canadian member, visited Washington to try for a settlement.

'I think this American fishery question bothers Sir John. I suppose it is ticklish business as Brother Sam may show fight.'

(Diary of Lady Macdonald, Jan. 4, 1871)

Sir John indeed was bothered. He knew that Britain as usual would pacify the Americans at the expense of its 'colony' and he feared, correctly, that Canadians would blame it all on him. Nevertheless, he had to at least try to win a fair deal for Canada. As negotiations dragged through the spring he stubbornly held out. But at last the Americans and British ground him down. Reluctantly he put his name to the one-sided Treaty of Washington that gave Americans fishing rights in Canadian waters for 10 years and free navigation on the St. Lawrence River canals. In return, Canada gained navigation rights to three remote Alaskan streams, free admission of Canadian fish to the U.S. market, fishing rights in some U.S. waters and $5,500,000.

Later Canada wrung compensation for the Fenian raids from Britain: a guaranteed loan for public works in return for obediently knuckling under at the Treaty of Washington. The Americans stuck Britain handsomely for the *Alabama* affair—$15,500,000. And later, too, the Canadian-American west coast boundary was fixed by arbitration. But none of this affected B.C's entry into Canada, fixed in 1870 and now awaiting only the formalities.

'Today British Columbia and Canada joined hands and hearts across the Rocky Mountains . . . At 12 o'clock last night there were manifestations of great rejoicing in the city. Bells were rung, guns fired, blue lights and Roman candles burned and crackers snapped. And people met on the streets and shook hands with and congratulated each other, and cheered and cheered and cheered . . . They were celebrating the Birth of Liberty.'

(*Daily British Colonist*, Victoria, July 20, 1871)

So the four tumultuous years ended on a happier note than their beginning. There was much still to do. Four more provinces to be drawn in, over 78 years. The incredible building feat of the CPR. Settlement, wars, depressions, French-English strife. Canadians were still very much the pioneers: Manitobans were advertising oxen in the lost-and-found columns; Barnard's Stage Coach line in Victoria on July 20 advertised a new 'fast' trip to Barkerville in the interior: exactly one week of steady travel. It was a long way to the 20th century, much less to a centennial. But the critical years were over.

Index to illustrations

People of the Longhouse

Douglas & McIntyre
·Vancouver · Toronto·

People of the Longhouse
How the Iroquoian Tribes Lived

Jillian & Robin Ridington
Illustrations by Ian Bateson

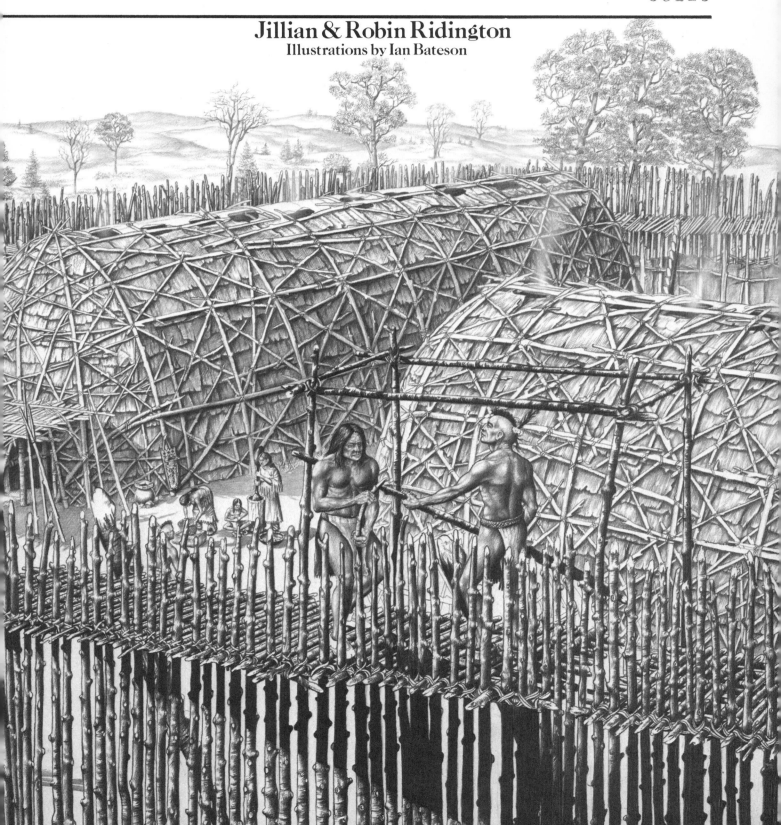

For our mothers, Ida Botham and Edith Farr
Ridington, who taught us our first lessons
and guide us still.

Douglas & McIntyre Ltd.
1615 Venables Street
Vancouver, British Columbia

Canadian Cataloguing in Publication Data

Ridington, Jillian, 1936-
   People of the longhouse

   (How they lived in Canada)
   ISBN 0-88894-357-1

   1. Iroquoian Indians — Juvenile literature.
I. Ridington, Robin, 1939-   II. Title.
III. Series.
E99.I69R53   j970.004'97   C82-091099-6

Book design by Ian Bateson
Typesetting by Domino-Link Graphic Communications Ltd.
Printed and bound in Canada by D.W. Friesen & Sons Ltd.

Contents

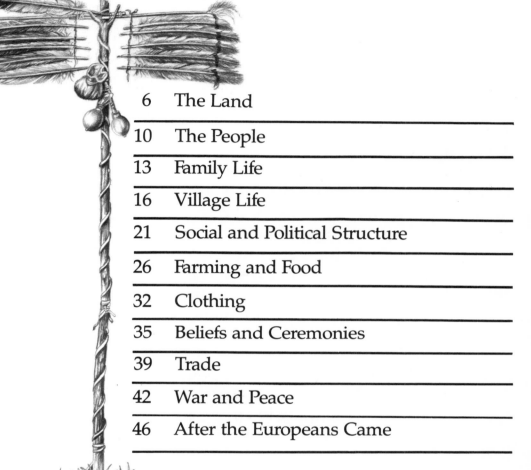

The Land

Long before Europeans came to this continent, Indians grew crops along a "corn belt" that stretched from Georgian Bay on Lake Huron south to Mexico, where the techniques and tools for growing corn, squash and beans originated about 5000 years ago. The northernmost of these native peoples, the Iroquoians, were Canada's first cultivators. They lived around the southern Great Lakes and in the St. Lawrence River valley, where the land was fertile and easy to work without metal tools.

Maize, as Indian corn was called, required 120 days without frost to ripen. Beyond Georgian Bay, the rocky soil and long winters made it impossible to grow maize. In the land of the Iroquoians, four well-marked seasons divided the agricultural year. Spring was a time of flowing sap and new buds. The earth thawed and was easily worked, ready to receive seed. Summer was dry, warm and long. July temperatures ranged in the twenties degrees Celsius. Before the corn was ripe, strawberries, raspberries and wild cherries could be gathered.

Autumn was a time of brilliant colours. The corn stalks turned from green to buff. The maple, birch and beech leaves blazed red and gold. Orange pumpkins and squash coloured the ground. Women harvested them together with the corn, late-ripening blackberries and sweet crab apples. In winter, the snow was deep. The

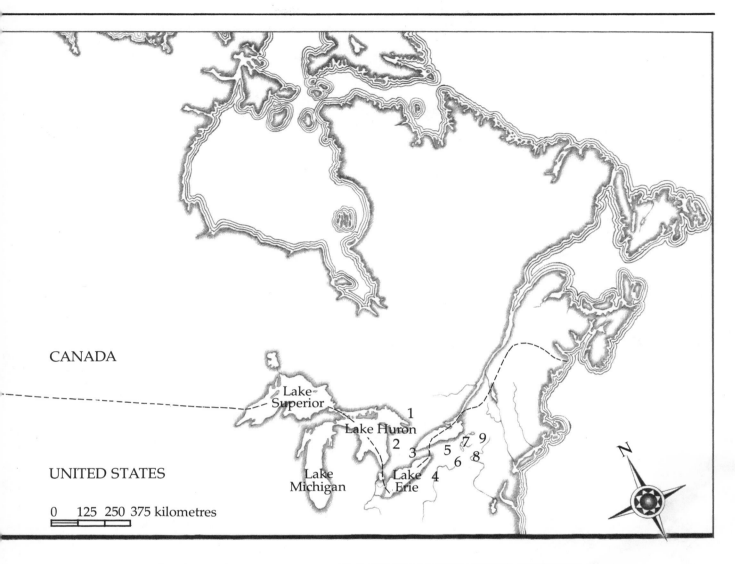

CANADA

Lake Superior

Lake Huron

1

2

3

5 7 9

6 8

UNITED STATES

Lake Michigan

Lake Erie 4

N

0 125 250 375 kilometres

Woman using a husking pin to remove the kernels from the cob of a fresh ear of corn. In front of her are some other plants that Iroquoians cultivated: pumpkins, squash, marrows and a variety of beans.

IROQUOIAN-SPEAKING GROUPS

1. Huron League

2. Petun (or Tobacco) League

3. Neutral League

4. Erie

League of the Iroquois

5. Seneca

6. Cayuga

7. Onondaga

8. Oneida

9. Mohawk

Huron trading party disembarking from its Algonkian birchbark canoes which are heavily loaded with baskets and clay pots full of dried meat, furs, clothing and ornaments

rivers and smaller lakes, frozen beneath the drifts, blended into the land. January temperatures averaged just below freezing. In this season of cold, people stayed close to their longhouse fires or travelled short distances by snowshoe.

No steep mountains divided the land. The birch, hemlock and pine of the northern forest blended into the maple, elm, ash and beech of the eastern woodlands. Gentle hills, easily climbed, provided high

points from which to spot an enemy or watch for returning kinsmen. Near such hills, and close to rivers or lakes where soil was sandy and water easily available, the Iroquoians built their villages.

The Great Lakes and hundreds of smaller lakes are joined by a network of rivers. Iroquoian men paddled these natural highways in bark canoes. These craft carried cargoes of corn, beans and animal skins to trade with friendly neighbours, or warriors intent on raiding enemy villages.

The fertile land made the Iroquoian way of life possible. Without their crops, the Iroquoians would have had to rely on hunting to feed themselves. Hunting people must follow their food supply and must devote most of their time to the pursuit of game. Farmers can grow their food in the same place year after year and can establish settled villages. Since women did the farming to produce the basic foods, Iroquoian men were free to travel, to trade and to raid.

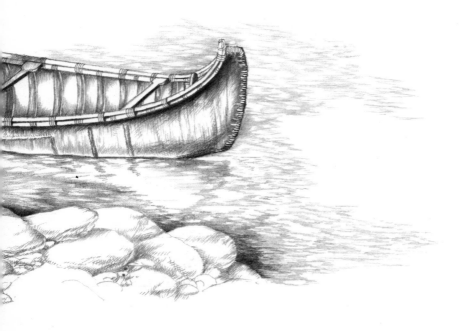

The People

For about 1000 years, the culture and languages of the Iroquoians dominated the central northeastern woodlands. These people spoke closely related Iroquoian languages, but each tribe had its own way of speaking and its own special customs.

The Iroquoians thought of their tribes as separate nations. The League of the Iroquois was called the Five Nations because it was made up of the Mohawk, Oneida, Onondaga, Seneca and Cayuga tribes. "Iroquois" was the name they were called by their enemies, the Ojibwa — and it means "poisonous snakes," but the five nations called each other by their tribal names in their own languages. At the time of its greatest strength, the League of the Iroquois had about 10 000 members.

The Bear, Cord, Rock and Deer nations who made up the Huron League lived in Huronia, the peninsula of land on the southeast corner of Lake Huron's Georgian Bay. The French called these people "Huron" which means "unkempt knave." The Huron preferred to be called "Wendat" which means "dwellers of the peninsula." With a population of between 20 000 and 30 000, the Huron formed the largest and most powerful of all the Iroquoian leagues. Although each nation had its own villages, they were close together, and all members of the Huron League hunted the forest between settlements.

South of Huronia and to the west were the lands of the Tobacco (or Petun) and the

Iroquoian adults loved children and were not strict with them; boys and girls were rarely punished and thought it a great disgrace just to be scolded

Neutral leagues. Although the soil in this southern area was not quite as easily worked as it was in Huronia, the climate was warmer. Tobacco thrived, and fruits and berries were abundant.

Farther to the southwest were the lands of the Erie or Cat people, so called because they often wore the skins of the bobcats that abounded in their territory. The Erie were the only Iroquoians not organized into a league.

The Neutral and Erie lived in the warmest part of Iroquoian territory, where the growing season was longest and the greatest variety of crops could be grown. They had the most people for the size of the lands they occupied. However, the total population of the Huron was greater because they had a lot more territory.

Although the Five Nations people were very like the Huron in many ways, members of the two leagues were enemies. This was, in part, simply because Iroquoian men saw raiding and warfare as the means of demonstrating their courage and proving their worth. Another reason was competition for trade routes.

In appearance, the Iroquoians were strong and lithe. They were taller than most Europeans at the time the two peoples first met. Because they had no written language, people developed excellent memories. They could remember long stories and speeches, and repeat them word for word even years after hearing them. The Iroquoians valued self-reliance, endurance and courage in both men and women. They could be cruel to their enemies but were gentle and considerate within their own groups.

Co-operation among those who lived in the same house, village or nation was essential. Each person knew that the group had to work together in order to survive. During the growing season, scouts and sentries were always present, because an enemy attack could endanger the food supply. In the biggest villages, groups of over 1000 people were able to live together, far more than could do so in nomadic hunting bands. These big groups could engage in elaborate ceremonies and games. They could also work together to build the huge longhouses in which they lived.

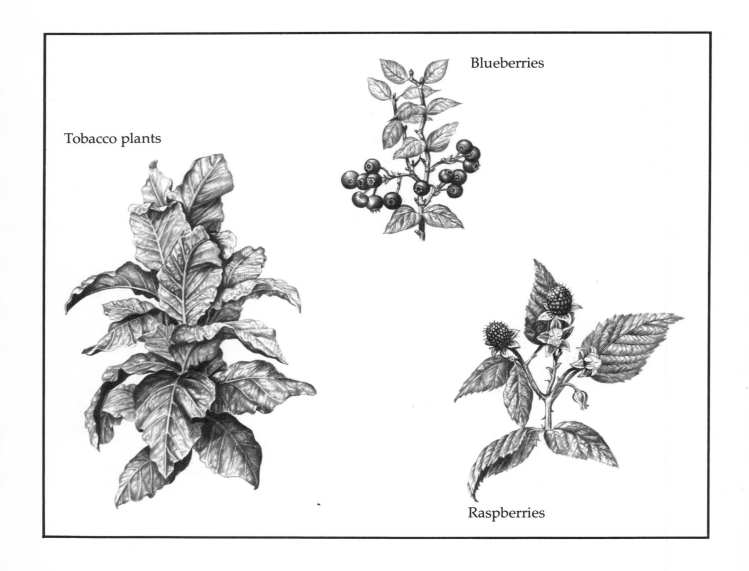

Blueberries

Tobacco plants

Raspberries

Family Life

Each Iroquoian longhouse was home to many families. These families were related to each other through their female members, since all children born to the women of a longhouse became members of a kin group called a clan. A clan was made up of people who could trace their descent through their mothers and grandmothers back to a common female ancestor. Male and female clan members of the same age group thought of themselves as being like brothers and sisters.

Every tribe had a number of clans, named for animals that were important to the people, such as the bear, wolf, turtle or hawk. A large clan might fill several houses in a village. The clan was headed by the clan matron, the oldest, most respected woman in it. She controlled the food supply, selected chiefs and arranged marriages for clan members.

In some tribes, a man's mother suggested a possible wife to him. If he liked her choice, she would speak to the woman's mother, who would then decide whether or not the man was a skilled enough hunter and warrior to marry her daughter.

Even after marriage, a woman's bonds to her clan were more important than her tie to her husband. Her world was centred on the longhouse and fields where she lived and worked with her mother and sisters. Any children born to her would belong to her clan. Children were always

The clan matron had a strong influence over life in the long-house. She controlled the food supply, selected chiefs and arranged marriages. Since a clan was thought of as a large family, marriage partners had to come from a different clan.

raised by their mother and her sisters and brothers, not by their father. Although a man moved into the longhouse of his wife's clan after marriage, he still spent a great deal of his time with his own clan, helping to raise the children of his sisters. Because a man's world was centred on the woods and waterways, he was often away from the village.

Childbirth proved a woman's competence and courage, just as success in battle proved a man's. She gave birth alone or with the help of an experienced older woman. If she cried or made noise during labour, she was considered cowardly and was scolded for setting a bad example.

The birth of a girl was greeted with joy, because she could give birth to more clan members and so ensure its strength. When a boy was born he was dipped into a stream right away; this was supposed to make him strong and fearless. Every baby was given a taste of animal oil right after birth to clean out his or her system. It also fed the child's guardian spirit which was believed to live in the soul from birth on.

Children had special names that identified them as belonging to a particular clan. The mother chose the name from a list of those owned by her clan and not being used by any living person. The child's name was confirmed at the next major festival.

As children grew up, they learned how to do things by watching and imitating the work of adults. When they were strong enough, toddlers helped to fetch wood and water. They carried the water in small pots that held about 500 mL. The pots looked like vases and were made of clay mixed with pounded stone or shells for strength.

Girls learned to make pots by forming very little ones which they used as toys. They rolled the wet clay mixture into a ball, then made a dent in this with a fist. To shape the pot, they slapped the outside with a wooden paddle, while turning the pot on their fist. The pots were dried in the sun, then baked in a hot fire. Iroquoians did not glaze their pots, but they did press patterns into the rims with corncobs, fingernails and other objects.

Girls were also taught how to pound dried corn into corn meal. They moved stout wooden pestles up and down in a mortar made from a hollowed-out tree trunk which was filled with dried corn.

Boys practised archery and other skills that would help develop their co-ordination, sharp sight and good aim to make them useful in the woods and warfare. They also learned to fish and snare animals by copying the men. At puberty, most boys went on a vision quest. They spent about two weeks in the forest, alone and without food, waiting for their guardian spirit to show itself. The spirit would foretell their future and give them a special song. Singing the song would give them courage and protect them in times of danger.

When girls reached puberty they cooked and ate their food alone, using special pots. Throughout their childbearing years, women observed these practices at each menstrual period.

Not all members of a clan were born into it. Adoption of both children and adults was common. In wartime, when many men were killed, clan matrons could adopt enemy captives so that their groups remained strong.

For the first year, a baby spent its waking hours in a cradleboard and was taken everywhere in it. The board could be propped against the wall of a house or hung from a tree near the women as they worked, or carried on the back of the baby's mother, sister or aunt. Cattail fluff served as diapers. At night the baby slept with its parents or in a hammock made of animal skins.

Village Life

Because the Iroquoian people were farmers, they did not have to move from place to place like the hunting people of the northern forest. Instead, they lived in villages near their fields. Large villages had palisades made of three rows of slender poles more than twice the height of a man. The poles were placed a few centimetres apart, reinforced with bark slabs, then woven together with branches. At the top were watchtowers, from which sentries kept a lookout. The palisades had only a single opening to make sneak attacks difficult. When tribe members in smaller villages were threatened, they took shelter in the fortified villages.

Villages had to be moved every 10 to 20 years, because the soil became worn out from farming and supplies of wood got used up. The new site was located as close as possible to the old one. The young men cleared the land and built new longhouses. House sites were in a random pattern so that fires could not spread easily.

Iroquoian homes were called longhouses because of their shape. They were often 40 m or more in length and 10 m in width. A village could have as many as 30 longhouses, with as many as 100 people living in each. At each corner of the building, the Iroquois used posts up to 10 cm across, sunk about a metre into the ground, with smaller posts in between. Perhaps 4 m above the ground, each corner post was notched to hold the four main

Inside a longhouse, the woman in the back is using a sieve made of hickory wood to sift the ashes out of kernels of popped corn. The woman to the right is grinding dried corn on a mortar in preparation for a meal. In the front, a mother is teaching her young daughter the art of pottery.

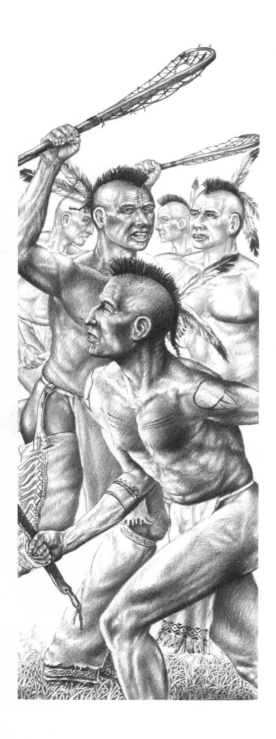

Men playing lacrosse. Lacrosse sticks were about 160 cm long and were made of wood; at the top was a basket woven from leather thongs. The balls were carved from wood or made of deerhide stuffed with hair.

cross beams. Slender poles were placed across the beams to form a framework for the roof. The sides were covered with overlapping large pieces of bark cut like boards, held in place by splints and rope made from bark. The front and back had openings which were fitted with bark doors set on wooden hinges, or hung with a bear or deer skin. Roof shingles were made of thinner pieces of bark. Holes were drilled in them so they could be attached to the roof frame with bark-fibre thongs. In the centre of the roof was an opening to allow smoke to escape, and light to enter.

Huron longhouses were similar. They had longer poles tied together at the top to form the roof. This gave their houses a more rounded shape. Also, Huron houses were tapered at each end and had storage porches inside the doorways.

In all homes, a long aisle ran down the centre, and cooking fires were made in this space. Along each side wall were rooms for each family, set apart by partitions made of hide or bark. Each family had its own metre-high sleeping or sitting platform, under which was stored food and utensils. For sleeping, bear skins were placed on top of it. Above the platforms were high lofts in which to store food supplies.

When people got together for a festival, the clans who shared each village played games and sports against each other. Lacrosse, now Canada's national sport, was invented by the Iroquois, who believed their ancestors gave them the game to develop the endurance and agility to become great warriors. Players raced the length of the field, using their sticks to carry the ball, to throw and catch passes, and to fling the ball into the goal. In summer, teams of men from different clans, villages or even nations played long, hard-fought games on grassy fields beside villages. For the big games held during major festivals, each team had hundreds of men.

In winter, they played snowsnake. It was usually a boy's game, but men played snowsnake as a team sport. They slid curved sticks over the snow to hit a wooden ball.

Winter was also the time for making and repairing clothes, goods and tools. The Five Nations made canoes from elm bark. They took large pieces of bark off a tree and removed the rough outside layer. Then they joined the pieces to form a canoe, pointed at both ends. A rim of ash wood strips was run around the edge, outside and in, and tied in place with bark twine. Ribs were also made of ash, set into the canoe at 20-cm intervals and secured under the rim. The canoes ranged in size from 3.5 to 12 m. The largest ones held over 20 men and were used on large lakes and big rivers. Smaller canoes held two or three people and were used on journeys where portages were frequent.

The women made twine from the inner bark of elm trees. They cut the bark into narrow strips, then boiled them in ashes and water so the strips would separate into threads. Men wove the threads into fishnets. Women made the threads into beautiful burden straps up to 5 m long. They braided the bark threads, then laid several braids beside each other and knitted them together with needles made of bone. The women wore such straps around their heads to help them support the weight of cradleboards, food baskets, or other burdens packed on wooden frames, which were like the frames of modern backpacks.

Men playing snowsnake. Both players and spectators often bet valued possessions, including weapons, tools, jewellery and clothing, on the outcome of the game.

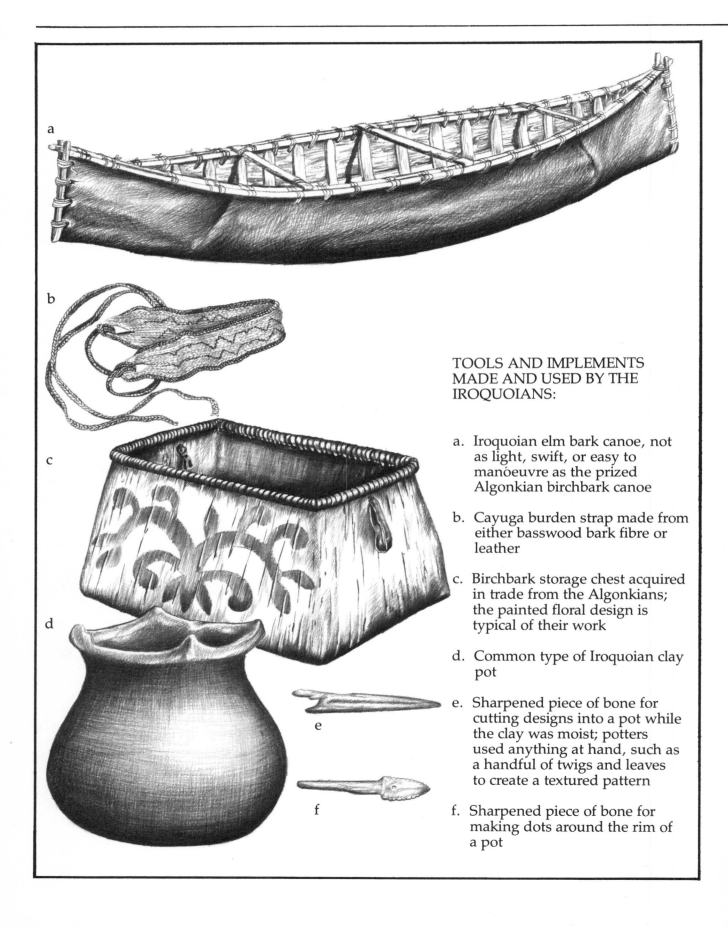

TOOLS AND IMPLEMENTS MADE AND USED BY THE IROQUOIANS:

a. Iroquoian elm bark canoe, not as light, swift, or easy to manoeuvre as the prized Algonkian birchbark canoe

b. Cayuga burden strap made from either basswood bark fibre or leather

c. Birchbark storage chest acquired in trade from the Algonkians; the painted floral design is typical of their work

d. Common type of Iroquoian clay pot

e. Sharpened piece of bone for cutting designs into a pot while the clay was moist; potters used anything at hand, such as a handful of twigs and leaves to create a textured pattern

f. Sharpened piece of bone for making dots around the rim of a pot

Social and Political Structure

The Iroquoian nations formed leagues because they wanted peace with their neighbours and trading partners, and allies to fight against common foes. The League of the Iroquois, the most famous one, was started over 500 years ago and still meets today. The Iroquois believe their league was founded by their ancestors Hiawatha and Dekaniwedah. Hiawatha's name means "he who seeks the wampum belt"; he was a different Hiawatha from the one in the famous poem by Henry Wadsworth Longfellow.

Hiawatha was an Onondaga whose family was killed in a blood feud. He grieved so much that he turned into a cannibal monster, consuming himself with anger and sadness. Wandering in exile, he reached a lake. As he stood on its shore, the sky filled with wild ducks. Landing on the water's surface, the ducks drank and preened, soaking their feathers in the water, until the lake was dry. Hiawatha saw small spiral shells on the lake bottom. To mark his grief, he picked up the shells and threaded them on the stalks of bulrushes.

Dekaniwedah, "the master of things," part god and part human, appeared. He told Hiawatha that he would help him to form a league of nations to prevent blood feuds and to spare people the terrible sadness of losing loved ones. The two travelled in a white canoe throughout the lands of the Iroquois, inviting the nations to join together in peace. The Mohawk were

Hiawatha picking up wampum shells from the bottom of the dried-up lake

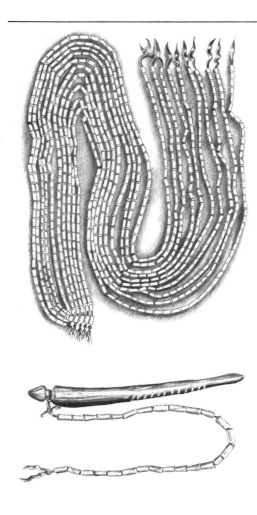

Top: the ten long strings of white wampum used in the great council
Bottom: the tally-stick and white wampum sent to all the member nations of a league to summon them to the great council meeting

the first to join, so they became known as "the elder brothers."

The Iroquois saw their league as having the same form as their homes. Like a huge longhouse, it was said to contain many fires, one for each tribal family. The people were to live together in peace, like one clan.

The constitution of the league later became a model for the constitution of the United States. All people had freedom of speech, freedom of religion and the right to hunt on the lands of member tribes. No Iroquois could shed the blood of any other Iroquois. If violence did occur, the victim (or the victim's family) had to be compensated by the payment of white wampum or goods to a value set by the league or tribal council. Witchcraft, treason and theft were crimes, and those who kept breaking the laws could be exiled. Exile meant that the guilty person was forced to leave the tribe. He or she would no longer have a home or family and, therefore, no protection or support. This punishment may seem harsh to us, but it was necessary in a society without jails, where co-operation was vital to the good of the people.

The constitution also set out the powers and responsibilities of the league, nation and village. The highest level, the great council of the league, was similar to Canada's parliament or the United States' congress. The tribal council was like a provincial legislature, and the village council was like a city council. However, at all these levels, representatives were chosen by the clans, not by voters living in the same area.

On the great council were 50 sachems or peace chiefs. Each nation had a different number of sachems on the council, but the numbers did not reflect the power of the nations in the league. The numbers depended on the agreements made when the nations joined the league and on the number of clans in each tribe. The nations with the most sachems could not control the council, since each nation had only one vote. The sachems from each nation had to agree on how to use their vote.

Once a year, the great council met in the land of the Onondaga, who were the "keepers of the council fire." They summoned the sachems to the meeting by sending messengers to the neighbouring Oneida and Cayuga. Each messenger carried a tally-stick with strings of wampum attached to it. The number of notches on the stick showed how many days it would be until the meeting. The Oneida sent a similar message to the nearby Mohawk, and the Cayuga sent one to their neighbours, the Seneca.

The great council made new laws and dealt with problems that concerned all the member nations. Each meeting lasted several days. Because all the sachems had to agree on each final decision, they made very long and eloquent speeches in order to try to convince the others of the rightness of their point of view. As each sachem spoke, he held strings of wampum in his hand to show that his words were true. When the wampum was taken from him and passed to the next speaker, it was a sign that the truth of his words was accepted.

A sachem served on the council for his whole life, unless he was removed by the matron of his clan. When a sachem died, the clan matron consulted with the other women in her group and chose a

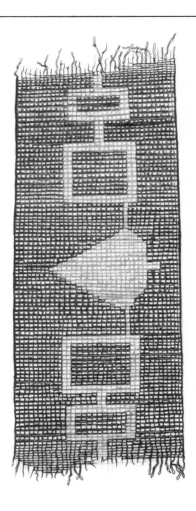

The Hiawatha wampum belt, commemorating the founding of the League of the Iroquois

replacement. Her choice was voted on by all the adult members of the clan. If he was approved, the new sachem took on the name and position of the former sachem.

Tribal councils included the sachems, the war chiefs and often the clan matrons. War chiefs were chosen by their clans for their courage and skill in warfare. The meetings were open to all members of the tribe. They had no vote but could influence decisions by making speeches. Tribal councils dealt with trade and warfare between their tribe and nations outside their league, and with crimes and punishments within their tribe.

Great council meeting of the five nations of the League of the Iroquois; the Mohawk speaker holds the wampum belt of unity while he addresses the council

Village councils usually included respected elders (both men and women), clan chiefs and matrons. Councils reached decisions through discussion and agreement. They co-ordinated village projects, kept order in the village, decided on compensation that wrong-doers should pay their victims, and set dates for rituals, ceremonies, dances and games.

The clan system gave the people a voice in all levels of government. The same clans could be found in several nations in each league. Members of one nation who were travelling through the lands of another tribe were treated as family members by people who belonged to their clan. This linked the nations in a league together.

Farming and Food

Cultivated fields lay outside every village. Land for farming was cleared by the men, who girdled all the trees in an area and waited until they died. This made it much easier to burn them as an aid to cutting them down with stone axes. Stumps were burned, and the roots were left to dry before being removed. Then the women levelled the ground around the remains of stumps with large, hook-shaped wooden rakes.

At planting time, the women soaked the seeds of corn (saved from the previous year's crop) in water to make them ready to sprout. The women in a clan worked together to help plant each other's fields. They used small wooden spades to form the soil into broad mounds about 30 cm high. Nine or ten holes were poked in the top of each mound, and seeds were planted in them. The mounds protected the seeds from the cold and discouraged weeds. In the same fields as the corn, many different kinds of beans were grown, especially kidney and lima beans.

Sunflowers were grown for the oil in their seeds, which was used for cooking. People also rubbed the oil on their bodies for protection from the cold or sun, and to soothe cuts or wounds.

Pumpkin, melon and squash seeds were sprouted in trays spread with light soil, then were moved outside and planted in the fields. In most tribes, tobacco was grown in small gardens. It was the only

Seneca method of braiding together ears of corn into a bunch for drying crop grown by men, who used it in ceremonies.

As the crops grew, little girls worked beside their mothers and aunts to weed the rows of plants. At harvest time, some women picked the ears of corn and put them into baskets. Others carried the full baskets to the longhouses. A third group cooked for the workers. The work was joyous, as the food supply for the winter was being made secure. In rest periods, they sang, played gambling games and told stories. At night, men worked with the women to bind the ears of corn into bundles which they hung from the roof beams of each longhouse.

When the corn was dry, the women and girls scraped the kernels off the cobs with a tool made out of a deer jaw. The dried corn was stored in bark casks. Beans were dried and kept in bark containers with lids. Squash and pumpkins were placed in deep, bark-lined pits in the houses, then covered with earth.

Women also gathered wild plums, grapes, cherries, berries and sweet crab apples. They picked many wild nuts including chestnuts, black walnuts and hickory nuts. Maple sap, gathered in the spring, was the only sweetener. This liquid was stored in seamless bark containers made in the shape of boats.

Men brought the clan its fish and meat. The Huron caught trout, sturgeon and whitefish in Georgian Bay, paddling their canoes 5 km out from shore to set their nets. Other Iroquoian nations relied less on fish than the Huron, as game was more abundant in their lands. The forests were home to black bears, elk, deer, rabbits and wolves, which were shot with bows and

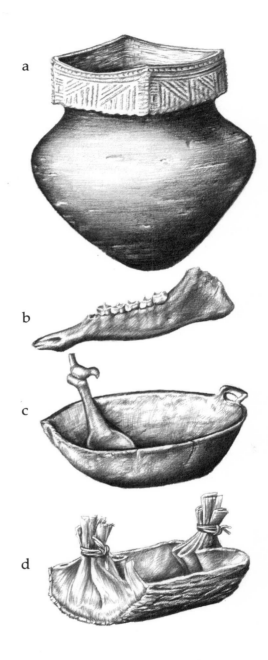

a. Clay cooking pot

b. Deer jaw scraper for removing dried kernels from the cob

c. Oneida wooden bowl for preparing or serving food or medicine

d. Seneca elm bark container for water or maple sap

arrows or caught in traps and snares.

To make a snare, a young tree was bent down and attached to the ground with a loop that would catch an animal by its hind legs. When a creature stepped into the loop, the tree was released and sprang up, suspending the catch in midair.

Game birds were plentiful. Wild turkeys, geese, ducks, herons, pigeons and partridges were caught in large nets hung between two trees. As many as 200 fowl a night could be captured this way, enough to feed all the people in a large village.

The clan's food stores were controlled by the women. When they felt that a war should not be fought, they prevented the men from going by refusing to provide food for the journey. If council meetings were not proceeding as they wished, they refused to prepare meals for the councillors.

A woman cooked food for her own family at the fireplace closest to her section of the longhouse. Water was boiled by dropping heated stones into a clay pot full of water. For slower cooking, the clay pots were hung directly over the fire.

Dried corn was prepared by boiling it first in water to which wood ashes were added. The lye in the ashes made the kernels swell and lose their hulls. The corn was then washed and cooked in soup with kidney beans, meat or boiled fish.

Men and women work together to clear the land and prepare new fields for planting. On the left, a man is chopping down a girdled, dead tree. On the right, men are building a small lodge out of saplings and bark for use as a shelter or storage.

Canada plum

Shagbark hickory

Sweet crab apple

Whitefish

American chestnut

Lake sturgeon

Gray partridge

Gray wolf

Great blue heron

White-tailed deer

Corn was also ground into meal and used to make a sort of bread. The loaves were small and flat, about 4 cm thick and 15 cm long. Sometimes dried berries or nuts were put in the bread. The loaves were boiled in water in large pots.

Most households ate only one large meal a day, usually in the late morning, though food was always available. Food was served from the pots with stone or wooden ladles. People ate with wooden or bark spoons from wooden bowls and drank from cups made of turtle shells or carved from wood.

a

b

c

d

TOOLS USED FOR CULTIVATING CROPS AND PREPARING FOOD:

a. Hoe blade made from an antler

b. Seneca double-pocketed elm bark basket to hold seeds for planting

c. Seneca husking pin

d. Seneca stone mortar and grinder

e. Wooden paddle for stirring soup

e

Clothing

Clothing serves as both protection and a form of decoration. The Iroquoians wore many kinds of clothing, all of it made from animal hides and furs. Women prepared the hides by removing the hair and flesh with stone scrapers. Then they soaked the hides in a solution of boiled deer brains to soften them. After drying, the hides were smoked to make them durable. Pieces of leather were cut to shape and sewn together with sinew that was threaded through holes pierced by bone awls. Skins of beaver, bobcat and squirrel were scraped only on the inside, leaving on the fur for warmth and decoration.

In summer, men and women wore loincloths of soft deerskin, held in place by a thong tied around the waist. Huron women also wore a skirt that reached almost to the knee. Both sexes often left their bodies bare from the waist up. They all wore moccasins on their feet.

When more protection was needed because of cold weather, men wore kilts and women wore longer skirts. Both sexes also wore leggings and jerkins with sleeves. These were held in place with leather thongs or burden straps tied around the body. In winter, they wore cloaks or robes made from bear, deer, buffalo or beaver skins.

They painted their bodies with geometrical designs or pictures of people and animals, which usually had a religious meaning. The paint was made by mixing natural pigments such as red ochre,

Man's summer clothing made of buckskin

Woman's summer dress made of buckskin

a. Deerskin leggings decorated with dyed porcupine quills

b. Deerskin shoulder strap or waist belt

c. Rattle made out of deer hooves worn strapped to the knee of a false face dancer

d. Seneca headdress of wood splints topped with eagle feathers

e. Deerskin cap placed inside the headdress

f. Man's moccasin decorated with dyed porcupine quills

g. Painted body designs, adapted from a painting called "The Death of Wolfe" by Benjamin West (1738-1820)

bloodroot and charcoal with sunflower seed oil. The Neutral and Tobacco inserted the pigments under their skin to produce permanent tattoos.

Iroquoians liked to wear ornaments such as woven sashes, fur and feather neckpieces, and feathered caps. They embroidered their clothing with dyed moosehair and porcupine quills. Everyday jewellery was made from common materials: feathers were made into earrings, animal teeth were hung as pendants on thongs, and segments of bone were strung into necklaces. On special occasions, both men and women wore bracelets and necklaces made from shell beads. Shells acquired in trade were a sign of wealth. Women also wore large shell plaques over their stomachs. A woman might wear as much as 5 kg of shell ornaments.

Hair styles were another important form of decoration. Women usually wore their hair hanging down the back in a single braid, bound with a thong. Men's styles varied. Iroquois warriors favoured the scalplock — a lock of hair dangling down the back of the neck — with the hair on the head shaved except for a strip down the middle from the forehead to the scalplock. Some wore close-fitting caps with a feather attached to the back. Huron men liked rolls of hair over their ears, or one side of the hair worn long and the other shaved. Some Huron men wore headbands made of snakeskin, with the snake's tail hanging down the back.

After contact with European traders, Iroquoians began to use woollen cloth rather than animal skins for their clothing. They embroidered these clothes with small glass trade beads in elaborate flower designs.

MAN'S WINTER OUTFIT: leggings, breechclout, kilt, moccasins and cloak

Beliefs and Ceremonies

Iroquoian people believed in many spirit forces created by a supreme being. Sky spirit forces took the form of wind, thunder, sun, moon and stars. Earth spirits took the form of plants and animals. All the spirit forces together were called "orenda," the Mohawk word for "song." Like a song, spirit forces flowed through all nature and controlled the weather and the lives of people, animals and plants.

They believed that anything they dreamed had to happen. If a warrior dreamed about being wounded, he would ask a friend to cut him slightly so that the dream would come true in this harmless way, rather than in battle. The shaman or medicine man dreamed more than an ordinary person and used the spirit forces that came to him in dreams to cure illness.

Each village had a special longhouse where councils and ceremonies were held. Many of the ceremonies were like plays, in which songs, speeches and dances told a story. The eagle dance tells the story of a boy who was carried off by the giant dew eagle, a powerful spirit bird. The boy returned to earth as a man with the power to cure illness. The bird was called the dew eagle because it collected a pool of dew in the hollow between its shoulders. When the thunder spirits that normally brought rain failed to come, the dew eagle showered the earth with dew to water the crops. The bird's power brought help for both sick people and plants.

Two of the four men taking part in the Seneca eagle dance

In the eagle dance, four young men from two different clans danced like eagles, while singers chanted and beat small drums carved from tree burls. The drums were filled with water and covered with ground-hog hide. The water gave the drums a high, clear tone. The dancers bent down to pick up small objects in their mouths in imitation of eagles feeding. Each held a horn rattle in his right hand to imitate the sound of birds scratching, and a feather fan in his left hand to represent wings with the power to sweep away evil. The sounds made by the rattles, drums and human voices helped people to contact the spirit forces.

Tobacco was often used in ceremonies because its smoke was thought to rise up to heaven, taking prayers with it. Tobacco was thrown directly on hot coals to produce smoke, or smoked in stone or clay pipes. Pipes were smoked with honoured guests, to end disputes or to strengthen friendships between tribes. The pipes were not passed from person to person as they were among the plains tribes.

Every year the Iroquoians held six or eight festivals. The most important was the midwinter festival. They feasted, played games, sang, danced, prayed and made speeches. They also gave thanks to the spirits of their most important food crops — corn, beans and squash — which they thought of as three sisters who were daughters of the mother earth. Other festivals celebrated the time of planting corn, the time when the corn was green, and the harvest of corn and other crops. They also celebrated the season when sap flowed in the maple trees, and the season when berries ripened. By watching the

A dreamer, carving a false face mask from a living tree, is chipping flint to make a carving tool

False face dancers driving out the evil spirits that cause sickness

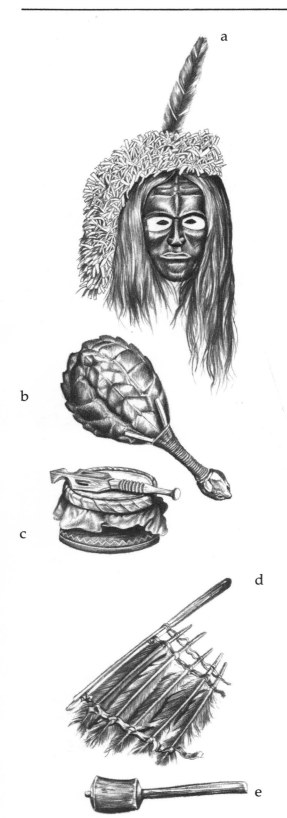

stars, they knew when to begin their festivals and when to plant and harvest crops.

Special ceremonies were put on by societies made up of people who had dreamed of the same spirit forces. One of these was the False Face Society, whose members were believed to have the power to drive out the evil spirits that caused illness. A man was called to membership in the society if a false face spirit came to him in a dream. He was accepted into it after he carved a mask to represent the spirit he had seen. The mask was carved into a living tree to give it the tree's power to heal itself. When the finished mask was cut out of the tree, it came alive with the power to heal sickness. Every spring and fall, false face dancers wore their masks and raided every longhouse. They crawled, jumped, hopped and struck the floor with turtle shell rattles. While they danced, they screamed and groaned. They had to be even more frightening than the evil spirits in order to drive out illness.

CEREMONIAL OBJECTS:

a. False face mask representing the spirit of the harvest

b. Turtle shell rattle used in the false face ceremony

c. Burl drum filled with water, used in the eagle dance

d. Five-feathered fan used in the eagle dance

e. Horn rattle used in the eagle dance

Trade

The men of all the Iroquoian-speaking nations engaged in trade with other nations in their leagues and with friendly neighbouring tribes. The Huron were the most successful traders since they were located on important canoe routes. Their territory was also particularly suitable for growing corn, so they grew a surplus to trade for meat and other foods which were scarce near their villages. They also got tools, clothing and ornaments. Huron traders were careful to maintain good relations with their trading partners. They often invited them to feasts and exchanged children with them to guarantee friendship.

Trading parties left Huron villages from early spring through summer and went out in every direction. A small group might consist of eight men travelling in two canoes. Large groups with up to a dozen big canoes, each carrying as many as 20 men, could travel as far as Lakes Michigan and Superior. The sachems of the Huron League decided how many young men should be allowed to travel, for some had to stay behind to protect their villages from enemy raiders.

From the Erie and Neutral to the south, the Huron got raccoon-skin robes, bobcat pelts, wampum, conch shells and calcium carbonate stones used in healing rites, and gourds in which to store oil. The shells may have come north from the Gulf of Mexico, in trade from tribe to tribe. From the Algonkian-speaking tribes to the north,

Huron trader exchanging dried corn for furs from an Algonkian hunter

the Huron got furs, dried fish, warm clothing and birchbark canoes. These canoes were prized because they were lighter and swifter than the Iroquoian canoes made of elm bark, for birch trees were scarce in Iroquoian territory. From the Cree who lived in the northern forest, the Huron got medicinal herbs and amulets. And from tribes living along Lake Superior and Lake Michigan, they got flint to make into tools, and copper. Copper was a rare metal, too soft to be made into tools, so it was used for ornaments in much the same way that we use gold today.

The Iroquois travelled and traded more on foot than by canoe. Their trading links with the Algonkian tribes were not as well established as those of the Huron. Their main trading partners were the Susquehannok and Delaware to the south, from whom they got shells. The Iroquois then traded some shells to the Neutral and Petun for tobacco and northern products received from the Huron. Because they had good access to shells from the coast, the Iroquois often used wampum as a form of money in exchange for goods.

Direct trade between the Iroquois and Huron did take place when there was peace, but the feuds between the two leagues made it unreliable.

In the early days of the fur trade, the Huron came to be important middlemen between the northern forest tribes and European traders. The Huron got furs from the Algonkians and traded them to the Europeans for metal tomahawks, metal knives, guns, glass beads and woollen cloth. The Iroquois traded beaver pelts from their own territory to Europeans in exchange for the same goods.

Iroquois with a burden frame secured to his back by means of a burden strap passed across his chest; for heavier loads he would also use an additional strap across his forehead

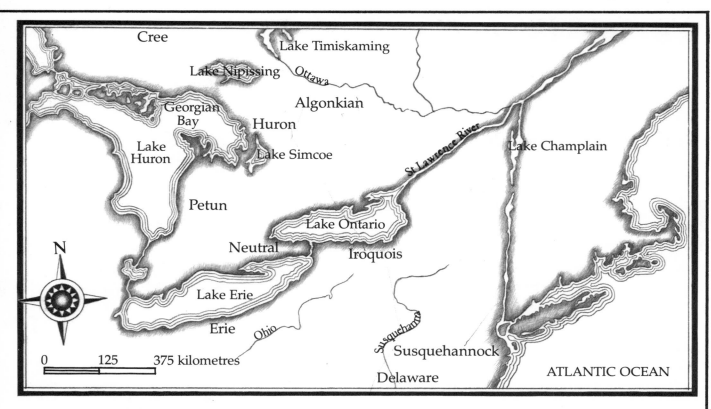

TRADING PARTNERS OF THE
IROQUOIANS AND THE WATER
SYSTEMS USED AS TRADE
ROUTES

a. Perforated wampum shells used
   as decoration and as a form of
   money for trade

b. Iroquois snowshoe made of
   hickory wood and laced with
   deerskin thongs

c. Burden frame with strap made
   of either bark fibre or deerskin

d. Algonkian birchbark canoe, a
   prized trade item

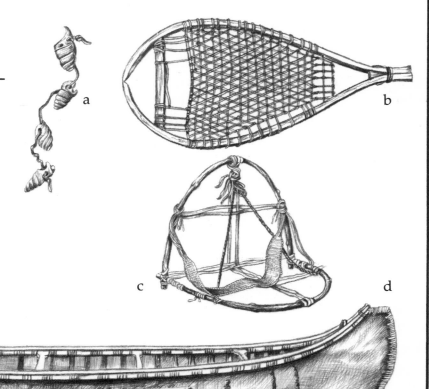

War and Peace

Being a warrior was important to a young Iroquoian man because raiding enemy villages gave him a chance to show courage, strength and knowledge of distant places. An older man, however, was more often called upon to become a sachem and showed his wisdom and diplomacy by leading councils for peace. Each showed good qualities in his own way.

Europeans fought wars to capture territory, gain trade or contest religious differences. But the Iroquoians fought blood feuds in which revenge and honour were more important than conquest. They made quick raids into enemy territory instead of fighting long battles.

A blood feud began when a person from one nation killed someone from a nation belonging to another league. It was a matter of honour to avenge the death by killing or capturing someone from the killer's nation or village. Until they did so, people in the victim's village felt weak and in danger.

Most raids took place between nations of different leagues. Raids were made only during the summer when swift travel was possible, as war parties often travelled long distances to raid an enemy village. Each warrior carried a bag of roasted corn meal mixed with maple sugar that would feed him for six to eight weeks on the trail. This trail food could be eaten by itself, or be cooked with fish and game caught during the journey.

Huron warrior wearing armour made from slats of wood

Until the Europeans gave them guns and metal tomahawks, warriors fought with clubs that had a round stone set into a carved wooden handle. They also used bows and arrows. The men made their own bows, which were over a metre long, out of wood. They hardened the wood with fire and shaped the bow with a shell knife. The bows, strung with deer sinew or cord made from hemp, required great strength to bend. Arrows were nearly a metre long, with a flint arrowhead at one end, and feathers twisted and tied at the other to make them revolve in flight. This gave their arrows much greater speed and accuracy than European arrows had at that time.

Warriors protected their bodies with shields made of wicker or bark, covered with hide. Some warriors, including the Huron, used light armour made from thin slats of wood, woven together with deerskin thongs. The shields and body armour were tough and flexible enough to stop stone-tipped arrows and deflect the blows of stone-headed clubs. They were also light enough to be carried over long distances. Often, warriors wore their finest shell necklaces and other ornaments on a raid. If pursued too closely they would drop these treasures and escape, while their enemies stopped to pick them up.

The greatest proof of a warrior's power was to bring back captives to his village. People believed that once an enemy was in their power, they regained the strength lost when their relative had been killed. Captives were often tortured in order to make their strength part of the strength of the village, rather than as punishment. A prisoner who was to be tortured and killed was allowed to give a feast in honour of his

Old Seneca sachem holding a pipe and peace council wampum

Iroquois warrior putting the final touches to the bow he is making from hickory wood

own death. The feast was sponsored by the family whose relative had been killed.

If a prisoner reminded his captors of the dead relative, they might spare his life and give him the name and titles of the man he replaced. Such an adopted prisoner might even join a war party against his own people since, by being captured, he would have lost honour among them.

The great council met to discuss disputes between league nations and to make peace with nations of other leagues. As a peace offering, each sachem smoked his own pipe and threw tobacco into the fire. Peace was often brought about because of great speeches in which a sachem would sing and act out many of his points. There were also special dances for making peace between feuding nations. At the conclusion of peace talks, representatives of warring nations exchanged presents such as shell ornaments, wampum and furs as a sign of goodwill.

WEAPONS OF WAR AND SYMBOLS OF PEACE

a. Cayuga bow

b. War club made from ironwood and a round stone

c. Wooden arrow with flint arrowhead and twisted feathers

d. Buckskin quiver to hold arrows

e. Shoulder bag for food, decorated with dyed porcupine quills and moosehair on black buckskin, probably Huron

f. Onondaga national wampum belt; the design represents an ever-growing tree to symbolize the perpetuity of the league

g. Wampum belt to summon the clan council to a meeting

h. Clay pipes used in ceremonies

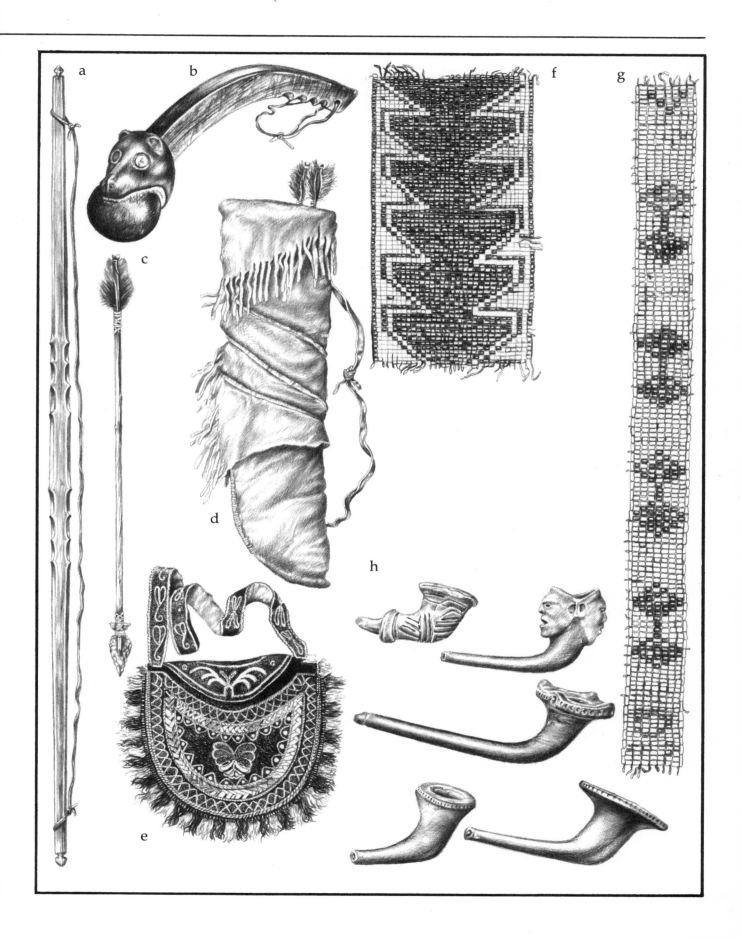

After the Europeans Came

In 1534, the French explorer Jacques Cartier saw corn growing along the banks of the St. Lawrence River, near the present-day city of Montreal. He was the first European to discover the prosperous farming territory of the Iroquoian people. After him came explorers, traders and missionaries who wished to bring European civilization to the native people, but whose presence actually brought about terrible destruction.

Thousands of native people died in epidemics of smallpox and other European diseases. And the bitter competition in the fur trade led to increased warfare among the Iroquoian leagues.

The Iroquois soon killed off most of the beaver in their territory and began raiding Huron villages for furs. In the winter of 1649, large Iroquois war parties invaded Huron territory. Only a few of the Huron survived the attack that followed.

The Five Nations of the League of the Iroquois became the Six Nations in 1722 when the Tuscarora joined. They fought in many more wars, the last in 1776 when the American colonies declared independence from Britain. The Seneca, Cayuga, Onondaga and Mohawk were persuaded to join the British, but the Oneida and Tuscarora joined the Americans. Thus, the long peace among the nations of the League of the Iroquois was broken by a war that really had nothing to do with them.

After the British lost the war, Joseph Brant, a Mohawk leader with a college education, led his people into southern Ontario. They settled on a reserve at Grand River, near the town of Brantford, since named for their leader. Other Mohawks established reserves at St. Regis on the St. Lawrence River, and Caughnawaga near Montreal.

The Iroquois nations that stayed in American territory had a difficult life. In 1800, a religious leader named Handsome Lake began to persuade his Seneca people to give up fighting and learn to use horses and plows. He received his power from dreams and visions. Many Iroquois still follow his teachings and meet in modern longhouses where they repeat his speeches from memory. They call themselves "The Longhouse People."

In the early 1900s, Mohawks at Caughnawaga began to work on high steel construction projects such as bridges and skyscrapers. They liked the work because it called for the same keen sight, courage and co-ordination that their ancestors valued. They are famous for their skill and bravery in this dangerous occupation.

Today, Iroquois people live on reserves in Ontario, Quebec and New York State. Many still think of themselves as a united people, so they believe they have the right to cross the Canada-United States border without restriction.

The Iroquois great council still meets, and the clan matrons still appoint sachems, but modern leaders such as band chiefs are elected. Members of the False Face Society continue to dance wearing their masks, in order to bring about good health for their people. The Iroquois are proud of a rich history that began long before the Europeans came to their country.

Joseph Brant, adapted from the portrait of him by the English artist Romney